SIMULATION GAMES 1.

PREVIOUSLY CALLED

USING
SIMULATION
GAMES

youth work guides

by
PAT BAKER
and
MARY-RUTH MARSHALL

JBCE

THE JOINT BOARD OF CHRISTIAN EDUCATION
MELBOURNE

National Library of Australia
Cataloguing-in-Publication entry

Baker, Patricia, 1932-
    Simulation games 1.

    3rd ed.
    Bibliography.
    ISBN 0 85819 582 8.

    1. Games in Christian education. 2. Simulation games in education.
    I. Marshall, Mary-Ruth. II. Joint Board of Christian Education of Australia and
    New Zealand. III. Baker, Patricia, 1932-   . Using simulation games. IV. Title.
    V. Title: Using simulation games.

268'.6

First printed under the title Using Simulation Games	1973		
Second edition	1974		
Reprinted	1982	1984	
Third edition, this title	1986		
Reprinted	1990	1991	1993

Cover: Stephen Stanley
Illustration: Michael Lindell
Printer: Brown Prior Anderson Pty. Ltd.

JB93/3302

Published by The Joint Board of Christian Education
Second Floor, 10 Queen Street, Melbourne 3000
Australia

CONTENTS

INTRODUCTION TO THE THIRD EDITION

Using Simulation Games made its first appearance back in 1973. It was a very limited edition, produced in duplicated form. The fact that it sold out very quickly encouraged us to produce an expanded second edition the following year. There have been numerous printings since then, with no change in content or appearance. So why are we trying to confuse you now by changing both the title and the cover?

We are not trying to confuse you at all. Our aim is clarity! *Using Simulation Games,* you see, had a sequel called *More Simulation Games,* and it was always our hope that some day there would be a sequel to the sequel. And there will be… within the next few months. But what do you call a sequel to a sequel so that people can remember which is which? We played around with the problem for a while, and concluded that a change of name would be the neatest way of dealing with it. So we have *Simulation Games 1 and Simulation Games 2,* with *Simulation Games 3* on the way… and more numbers available for the future. To celebrate the new series we commissioned Stephen Stanley to design bright new covers for all three books.

Much has happened in the world since 1973, yet we believe that the games in *Simulation Games 1* are still quite relevant. The issues with which they deal are still with us, and the games can help groups as they grapple with them. One change we have made from previous editions is the deletion of the section on 'other accessible games' — the problem being that most of them are no longer available or accessible! If we were actually rewriting the book at this time, there is another change that we would make — and that is in terms of inclusive language. To refer to a player as 'he' was quite acceptable 13 years ago. Now it grates, and you will find much more careful use of language in *Simulation Games 3.*

We enjoyed putting this book together. We hope that you will enjoy using it. And if you move on from using these games to designing your own, we would be interested to hear about them.

I can only sign my own name to this, as Mary-Ruth is now living and studying (and very likely gaming) in the United States, but the production of this book was very much a joint effort.

PAT BAKER
April 1986.

1

An introduction to games and their uses

What are simulation games?

What, indeed? More than one book on the subject hedges around this question, maintaining that it is more satisfactory to become involved in the game itself than to try to define it. While that may be true, it seems desirable at least to make an attempt at a definition.

No two writers use the terms "game" and "simulation" in precisely the same way. Some make sharp distinctions, while others use the terms interchangeably. The rule of thumb we intend to follow is this: if it lines up with the definitions given below, we call it a "simulation" or a "game" — or maybe a "simulation game". If it does not really simulate some form of reality, or if it doesn't have the usual elements of a game, we refer to it as an "exercise".

The two essential elements of simulation games are that they are *simulations* and that they are *games*.

A dictionary defines "simulate" as "to give the appearance or effect of". A simulation is an imitation or representation of something else, an operating model of a physical or social situation. (A good example of a physical simulation is Capsim, the capsule simulator used in training astronauts for space missions.)

In simulation, reality is reduced to manageable proportions. What in real life may be an extremely complex situation is simplified and condensed; non-essentials are omitted.

The simulations with which we are concerned are also games, involving many of the elements which we associate with other kinds of games: there are goals to be achieved, rules to be observed, usually some form of competition — and they are fun to play!

Types of games

Simulation and other educational games fall into two basic categories: board games and role-play games. The format selected usually depends on the subject, and the purpose or group of people for which the game is designed.

Board games. These are built around a gameboard on which most of the action takes place. They are similar to Monopoly or Ludo. (Monopoly, incidentally, could be called a simulation game.) By the end of the game, players have seen the course of development graphically represented on the board.

Role-play games. This basic structure is used primarily in games that teach processes involving negotiation, bargaining, compromise; in general, human interaction. A scenario sets the scene for the action, and each participant has a specific role to play. This may be clearly set out in a role profile, or left to the individual to develop from a broad general outline.

Some games combine the two techniques described above. These may be characterized as *hybrid games*. Play may be primarily on a board, but with some negotiations taking place. Or the only function of the board may be to record the results of decisions or other interaction which is taking place.

There are also *pencil and paper* games which may have some of the characteristics of role-play games.

The purposes of simulation games

Conflict and change are part of our way of life. How can we confront and deal with conflict? How can we anticipate the effects of possible changes? Games can help us to do both these things.

A game may thrust us into a conflict situation — perhaps one that we would try to avoid in real life. In the game there is no escape. We have to come to terms with the situation and the other people involved. We have to make choices and decisions. And we have to live with the results of those choices.

What games provide, perhaps uniquely, is the opportunity to deal with complex problems in concrete ways. Often a game enables us to get the "feel" of a situation in a way that would be impossible for us in real life. And because the game reduces reality to manageable proportions, we are able to act with a greater sense of purpose and understanding.

Games also provide opportunities for experimenting and taking risks. They allow us to try things out: different behaviour, new solutions to familiar problems, different ways of organizing our simulated environment.

Each game has its own specific purposes, but we may make a general summary of the purposes of simulation games along these lines:

1. To become aware of existing views on an issue.

2. To understand the social, religious, political, and economic aspects of the situation.

3. To understand the feelings of those in the situation.

4. To analyze possible outcomes, or actual historical ones.

5. To generalize factors and apply to other cases.

The educational values of simulation games

1. Most games demonstrate the advantage of co-operative effort (though a strong competitive element is often involved).

2. They develop empathy, with the possibility that the player will develop sensitivity to and under-standing of the person whose role he has assumed.

3. Games help develop the ability to analyze the essential elements in a situation.

4. Games provide a chance to experience the situation, not merely to hear or read about it.

5. Players learn that there is a causal relationship between their behaviour and the outcome of events.

6. Games allow for feelings to be expressed, even hostile ones.

7. Players can explore the possibilities of affecting (changing) their environment.

8. Players are involved in relevant inquiry, questioning values in a non-threatening atmosphere, thereby learning to think critically and creatively.

9. Games provide high motivation for learning.

10. Players may gain insight into their own behaviour, thereby assisting in their personal growth. They may also gain insights into their relationship with others.

11. Consequences of decisions can be immediately observed and evaluated.

12. Players learn to take responsibility for their own decisions and actions.

13. Games provide a non-judgmental learning experience. (At least, the players are not judged externally.) Everyone learns from the experience, losers as well as winners.

14. What counts is actions, deeds, moves; not rhetoric, acceptable statements, vows or promises.

The most vital part of the learning process in simulation games is the evaluation at the end: the "de-briefing", "de-roling", or post-mortem period. It is at this point that most of the real learning takes place. The two key questions are: what decisions were taken during the game and what were their effects?

Any disadvantages?

Criticism has been levelled at simulation games on the grounds that they:

1. Over-simplify.

2. Fool players into thinking that they know all there is to know about a given topic.

3. Allow players to manipulate the lives of others without being affected by the constraints of real life.

4. May have the "life-likeness" of a situation heightened or marred by the personalities of the players.

5. May have only a short-lived effect on the attitudes and life-style of the players.

6. Could teach the advantages of unscrupulous self-interest.

7. Work upon the emotions (that is, "simulate") to such a point that players become over-involved.

While these criticisms may be valid, they may be applied equally to other learning approaches. Certainly we ought to keep them in mind lest our enthusiasm for games blind us to possible drawbacks. In particular we should be prepared to take these points into account when evaluating any game.

The use and misuse of games

One of the dangers in using simulation games is that they can become interesting ends in themselves. We decide to include a game in our group's programme because it is available, rather than because we believe that it will help us to come to grips with an important issue. We misuse simulation games when we treat them as novelties or interesting programme fillers. Our decision to use a particular game should stem from a concern for the issues with which it deals, not because it "sounds like fun".

While most games are suitable for "single-shot" programmes, their most effective use often comes when they are used as part of a broader programme.

A game might be used to introduce a topic which the group will be studying over a number of weeks. You would expect the game to acquaint the participants with the broad outlines of the problem at hand, and to motivate them in a desire to become more deeply involved in studying the issues and in seeking solutions. Alternatively, a game might be the culminating activity of a programme, pulling together the elements that have gone before.

Let's take some examples. "I'm Superior . . ." (pages 12—13) could give an effective start to a study of racial prejudice in this country. Alternatively, it could be used after the group members have made some investigation of the situation, to bring home to them the implications of what they have discovered.

Quite a number of groups have made use of a meal to point up the gap between rich and poor nations in terms of living standards. The group is given no warning of what is to happen. When the meal is to be served they are divided into sub-groups. The smallest group is given an elaborate and satisfying meal. Other groups receive much smaller quantities of far less attractive food. Some have nothing at all. Such an experience, coming after a study of the gap between rich and poor nations, can really bring the subject to life.

2

Glossary of terms

SIMULATION   an imitation or a representation of an actual physical or social situation reduced to manageable proportions to serve a specific purpose.

SIMULATION GAME   a series of activities in a sequence in which players participate in a "simulation" which (1) has stated rules, (2) usually involves competition, (3) leads toward an objective.

SCENARIO   a briefing of the situation up to the moment of the game.

ROLE-PROFILE   description of a specific player's objectives, rationale, and resources, with helpful hints towards strategy.

GAME DIRECTOR   (sometimes called game leader, gamemaster, or referee) the person in charge of the game, responsible for its proper functioning.

DE-BRIEFING
(also called de-roling)   the period at the end of the game when players drop their roles and become themselves again. This sometimes merges with —

EVALUATION   the discussion which follows the game.

3
Directing
a simulation

In all simulation games, the game director plays an important part. He or she must be thoroughly conversant with all phases of the game being played: its purpose, its schedule (that is, what happens next), the roles of the players, the type of interaction that will take place, the points at which conflict is to be expected, the likely outcomes, the probable learnings.

It is important that the director remain "outside" the game in the sense that he/she does not take part as a player (although in some games he/she may be required to act as banker or messenger). The functions of the director are to direct, and to be aware, at all times, of what is going on.

The director's function may be described in three phases: briefing, oversight, and de-briefing and evaluation.

1. **Briefing.** The director first of all introduces the game, explains as much as needs to be explained of its purposes, assigns roles, distributes and interprets materials, and answers questions for clarification. This demands a thorough knowledge of the game and its purposes. Instructions should be clear and to the point. The director should know which questions are to be answered, and which should be left to be answered by the game itself.

2. **Oversight.** It is vital that the director knows what is happening at all stages of the play. He/she should be particularly aware of any conflicts that are building up. Conflict is a part of the game and usually serves a good purpose, but a game may be cut short if the situation seems to be getting out of control.

In most cases the director is also responsible for the timing of the game. All pre-arranged limits should be strictly observed.

A director who is well up with a game may sometimes decide to help the action along a little if it appears to be lagging. This can be done by introducing new material in the form of a message to one or more players. (Some games make provision for this by providing special materials. An alert director can do it by devising his/her own special input.)

3. **De-briefing and evaluation.** It is the director's responsibility to help the players at the end of the game to sort out and assimilate their experiences.

The first step is to de-role the players. They are no longer allowed to be the characters whose roles they assumed. Name tags or other distinguishing marks are removed. The players are themselves again. The director should take care that the hostilities of the game are not permitted to spill over into the evaluation period.

Most game instructions set out the kinds of questions which may be used to draw out the players' experiences. The most important ones are concerned with what happened in the game and why. Players should be encouraged to talk about their feelings, frustrations, and decisions, and also about what they could have done to improve their role performances. Finally, it is important that the players be helped to transfer their experiences in the simulated situation to that situation as it exists in real life.

4

Try these for a start!

Now we get down to the nitty gritty: complete playing instructions for 24 games. They are —

I'M SUPERIOR AND COULDN'T BE PROUDER — a role-playing game about prejudice and discrimination. Number of players: 6 plus.

ARMS RACE — a role-playing game about international tensions. Number of players: 6 plus.

POVERTY — a role-playing game about the pressures which society exerts on the poor. Number of players: 12 plus.

CRISIS IN THE CHURCH — a role-playing game about conflict in a local congregation. Number of players: 8 plus.

CRYSTAL PISTOL — a role-playing game about conflict between youth and adults. Number of players: 30—50.

THE GAP — a role-playing game about the inability of people in unskilled and semi-skilled jobs to rise out of their situations. Number of players: 8 plus.

IMMIGRANTS — a role-playing game about the problems of immigrants. Number of players: minimum of 12 "staff", plus 20 or more players.

FAMILY CHARADES — a role-playing game highlighting relationships within a family. Number of players: 6 plus.

PAY-OFF — a game of conflict and trust. Number of players: 4—20.

GETTING THERE! — a board game about ways and means of achieving desired goals. Number of players: 3—8.

THE MILK RUN — a role-playing game concerned with decision-making. Number of players: 6 plus observers.

PROJECT ECONOMY — a long-term (2—6 days) role-playing game to help participants experience the dynamics at work between rich and poor. Number of players: 20—50.

MANA — a board game about youth in a multi-racial society. Number of players: 4—10.

THE CONVICT GAME — a board game to introduce players to the nature of the convict system in the eastern Australian colonies between 1788 and 1853. Number of players: 3—10.

POOR MAN'S CAKEWALK — a board game about some of the development problems of the Third World. Number of players: 2—10.

MONOPOLY — a new idea for using the familiar board game, focusing on economic discrimination. Number of players: 2—6.

FOCUS — a hybrid game in which players are confronted with some of the tensions and problems faced by indigenous leaders in Papua New Guinea. Number of players: 3—6 (or more if teams are used).

CHRISTLIFESTYLE — a hybrid game concerning Christian conduct in a variety of situations. Number of players: 3—10.

CAMP LEADERS' TRAINING GAME — a hybrid game to prepare leaders for situations which may arise during a camp. Number of players: 3—10.

SURVIVAL SHELTER — a pencil and paper game concerned with decision-making and the expression of values. Number of players: 3 plus.

SPREE! — a pencil and paper game concerned with the use of money. Number of players: unlimited.

SWIM — a pencil and paper game concerned with programme planning to achieve desired goals. Number of players: 1 plus.

THE POPULATION BOMB — a pencil and paper game about the population crisis. Number of players: 3 plus.

YOUTH WORK CARD SORT — an exercise concerned with identifying weaknesses in current programmes. Number of players: 3 plus.

For page references see page 3.

I'm SUPERIOR

and couldn't be prouder

I'm Superior

A simulation game by Tom Morgan, reprinted from YOUTH PROGRAMS, Volume 19, by kind permission of The American Lutheran Church, Division of Youth Activity.

This simulation offers an opportunity to experience what prejudice and discrimination do to both the majority and the minority group. The simulation may be seen either as an experiment in human relationships or as a programme of emphasis on race and cross-cultural relations.

Procedure

At the beginning of the meeting the leader divides those present into two unequal groups. One is the majority or superior group, and the other the minority or inferior group. About one-third of those present should be in the minority group.

The criterion used to distinguish between the inferior and superior people should be some inherited characteristic like brown or blue eyes. Select a quality that puts about one-third of the people in the minority classification. Other criteria that can be used are: freckles, curly hair, names beginning with A–F, born in winter (June–August).

After the majority people are separated from the minority people, read the rules for each group.

Rules for the behaviour of majority people

1. Always refer to the minority people as "goons" or "scum".

2. Take and defend your proper place in life and be proud of your status.

3. Make sure that the minority people do not get away with more than they should.

4. Call attention to anything that a minority person does that is out of line.

5. Occasionally nag or harass the minority people for no particular reason at all.

Rules for the behaviour of minority people

1. Never speak to a majority person unless spoken to.

2. Always refer to a majority person by using the title "Mr" or "Miss" before his name, or address that person as "Sir" or "Ma'am" when speaking to them.

3. Always sit on the floor or ground when in the presence of superiors.

4. If a majority person is coming your way, make room for him to pass.

5. Never raise your voice to a majority person.

6. Stay in the proper "goon" or "scum" areas.

7. Never drink from the same cup or fountain as a majority person.

8. If food is being served, always wait until the majority people have finished eating before you eat at all.

Doing the simulation

After the rules are read and it is clear what is expected of both groups there are two ways of carrying out the simulation:

1. The regular business of the group can proceed as usual. It might include a devotion, Bible study, topic presentation, discussion, or business meeting, or any combination of these things in the typical kind of meeting of your group. Refreshments can be served. Throughout the meeting the rules are observed. It would be particularly interesting to have a Bible study on "love" and see how the majority group rationalizes the rules that govern their treatment of the minority people.

2. Each group may be given 15 to 20 minutes to prepare their arguments for a dialogue. The majority people list the reasons why it is quite logical (maybe even biblical) that the rules against the minority people be imposed. The minority group lists the reasons why they should not be discriminated against. When each group has prepared its case, they are brought together for a discussion. The discussion is carried out under the rules which have been imposed. The leader may have to prompt one side or the other to get things moving.

After the simulation

The leader will call a halt to the simulation when he feels the groups have carried on an adequate discussion. It may not be a normal type dialogue because of the rules which have been imposed but hopefully members of both groups will have had moments when their roles were "real" to them.

It is extremely important that enough time be allowed to "blow off" and talk it out! Steer the evaluation away from the "sides" that were taken during the dialogue or programme (the groups will easily fall back into the role-playing). Keep asking people how they felt during the simulation, and what insights they got about prejudice, anger or hatred. If minority people felt angry, consider how much anger there might be in people who have known years of prejudice. And just how close to the surface does anger dwell in most of us? Evaluate how much insight the majority group demonstrated in rationalizing the unfair rules imposed on the minority. Did they see parallels with any situation in this country today? Did the participants come to understand any more clearly how injustices against minority groups can become an unquestioned part of the rules that govern society? And who makes and maintains the rules?

WARNING: In any group-role-playing activity it is possible that hostilities may develop between people which are not easily or quickly forgotten. The "cooling-off" period is important! It is also important that the "competition" not be continued after the evaluation has begun! The game director can help by referring to the players and their roles in the third person. For instance, "How did the majority player feel?" rather than, "How did you feel?"

Arms Race

Reprinted with permission from "Let's Play War" by William E. Irwin, in SHARE: A PAPER FOR TEACHERS AND LEADERS, August 1972. Copyright © 1972, United Church Press.

This game tests your "theology" of war. You will discover how secrecy, fear, and ignorance affect human behaviour. The game simulates the situation of three countries engaged in a nuclear arms race. As production of bombs and missiles begins, an unhealthy competitive spirit is generated. Midway in the process an opportunity is provided for the countries to negotiate. The ways in which the participants react to this situation is instructive. Participants immediately see the comparison with the arms buildup in the world today. Arguments arise in each country about how to build bombs and how to negotiate. The frustrations of getting people to agree on anything are discovered. If a "nuclear war" is fought, as it usually is, a winner is decided upon on the basis of the fewest killed. The questionable value of this type of winning is readily seen.

After the war, discussion and comment should flow freely. There may be complaints of unfairness in bomb building capacity, which of course is built into the game. Groups must face their own beliefs about what they value in life, about people and how they should function toward one another in today's world.

The game

Provide three boxes containing materials for building bombs and anti-ballistic missiles (ABMs). Box A contains paper, scissors, straight pins for joining the paper parts, and a prototype of a bomb. Box B contains the same items except that a stapler is included instead of pins. Box C is the same except that it provides glue to join the paper parts. Thus each box contains a different capability for building bombs and ABMs.

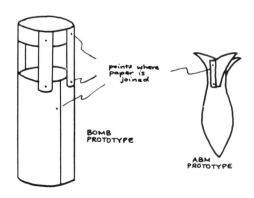

points where paper is joined

BOMB PROTOTYPE

ABM PROTOTYPE

● Divide into three groups at work tables or in widely separated or screened off areas of the room. Have a game leader or referee and three checkers who check group activities and carry messages to the referee.

● Announce that you will be having a nuclear war. Everyone must remain in his area unless he has permission from the referee to leave. Emphasize secrecy. No group may know what the others are doing. Distribute boxes and Instruction 1.

> **Instruction 1:** In the box is a prototype of a bomb and materials for building it. Build as many as you can until the referee says stop. The bombs must be the same size as the prototype.

● After ten minutes distribute Instruction 2. Allow another ten minutes for work. Meanwhile set up chairs in the centre of the room for negotiations.

> **Instruction 2:** With this sheet you will receive a prototype of an ABM (anti-ballistic missile). Your country now has bombs to hit the other two countries and the capability of making ABMs that can explode bombs before they reach you. One bomb delivered to another country kills 10 million people (10 megadeaths). One ABM will save one million people in your country. (The bombs have multiwarheads and are more effective than ABMs, but ABMs can be built faster than bombs.) Your group must decide whether to make bombs for offence or ABMs for defence. You don't know what the other countries are doing. They may be able to build faster or slower than you. The winner will be the country with the fewest deaths.

● After ten more minutes distribute Instruction 3. Only two representatives may use the negotiating area at any one time: one from each of two countries. This builds tension.

> **Instruction 3:** Negotiations may stop the arms race. You may arrange with the referee to talk to *one* other country at a time. Send your representative to the referee, to contact the other country. You may make any plans you wish. If "peace" is to be declared the negotiators should arrange for a public announcement to be made.

● After ten more minutes distribute Instruction 4. (If negotiations have been successful, war is unnecessary and the game ends without this distribution.) The checkers collect the reports and tabulate them. (See score sheet.)

> **Instruction 4:** War has been declared. Count your bombs and ABMs. Decide how many bombs you will send to each of the other two countries. Give your report to one of the checkers. Total ABMs . . . . . . Bombs sent to A . . . . . . to B . . . . . .

● Announce the winner. Call the groups together and discuss their reactions. Be sure to discuss: Was war necessary? Why did it happen?

SAMPLE SCORE SHEET

Country	ABMs made	Bombs made	Bombs sent	Bombs rec'd	Megadeaths possible	Megadeaths saved	Total killed
A	20	15	B 8 C 7	16	160	20	140
B	30	12	A 6 C 6	18	180	30	150
C	15	20	A 10 B 10	13	130	15	115

POVERTY

This game is designed to give the participants some experience of the pressures which society exerts on the poor and underprivileged.

Playing instructions based on description of a game in COLLOQUY, March, 1969.

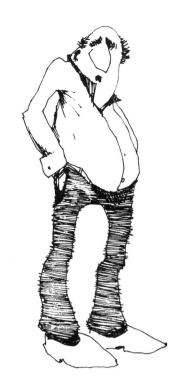

Number of players: Twelve or more, plus game director.

Materials required

All kinds of material and junk for constructing collages:

    poster paper
    newsprint
    paste
    scissors
    illustrated magazines
    foil
    tissue paper
    pipe cleaners
    drinking straws
    string
    ice cream sticks
    feathers
    matches
    paper doilies
    felt-tipped pens
    old costume jewellery
    gummed stars
    sequins
    used greeting cards

Play money, or chips to represent money.

Copies of instructions for participants.

An envelope for each player.

Preparation

Prepare an envelope for each player. This should contain the appropriate instructions for that player, plus the amount of play money with which he will start the game. The envelopes should be numbered and distributed in the following order:

1. CITIZEN (no money); 2. CITIZEN (no money); 3. CITIZEN (3 units of play money); 4. CITIZEN (3 units); 5. CITIZEN (6 units); 6. CITIZEN (10 units); 7. CITIZEN (15 units); 8. SHOPKEEPER (10 units); 9. WELFARE WORKER (10 units); 10. POLICE OFFICER (5 units); 11. CLERGYMAN (10 units); 12. ORGANIZER OF THE POOR (no money); 13. SHOPKEEPER (10 units); 14. CITIZEN (no money); 15. CITIZEN (6 units); 16. WELFARE OFFICER (10 units); 17. CITIZEN (12 units); 18. POLICE OFFICER (5 units); 19. SHOPKEEPER (10 units); 20. CITIZEN (no money); 21. CITIZEN (20 units); 22. CITIZEN (6 units); 23. CITIZEN (no money); 24. CITIZEN (10 units); 25. CITIZEN (no money); 26. WELFARE OFFICER (10 units); 27. CITIZEN (6 units); 28. POLICE OFFICER (5 units); 29. CITIZEN (3 units); 30. CITIZEN (3 units); 31. SHOPKEEPER (10 units); 32. POLICE OFFICER (5 units).

NOTE: Players 1—12 are essential. With more than 32 players, work through the list again. You may like to add a NEWSPAPER REPORTER (10 units). This role could be assigned at any point after the first twelve.

To simplify starting procedures, each envelope should be marked "citizen", "welfare worker", or whatever.

Instructions for participants:

CITIZENS

You have half an hour in which to produce a collage. (A collage is a work of art consisting of paper and other objects pasted on a base sheet of poster paper or newsprint.) At the end of the thirty-minute playing period, *every citizen must have a collage to hang on the wall.* No excuses will be accepted. The materials you will need for the job are on sale at the shops. Your total financial resources are enclosed in this envelope. If you get into financial difficulties you may (a) apply to a welfare worker for relief, (b) ask the church for help, (c) ask the shopkeeper for credit, or (d) try to get a job in one of the shops or helping a richer citizen.

SHOPKEEPERS

Each of the citizens must produce a collage within the thirty-minute playing period. They must buy the materials they need from you and the other shopkeepers. The money enclosed in this envelope is for use as change. The citizens have varying amounts of money available (ranging from 20 units to nothing at all). Your aim should be to make as much money as possible during the course of the game. You may set your own prices, and change them at any time. You may give credit if you wish. You may also hire assistants if needed.

POLICE OFFICERS

You are responsible for the maintenance of law and order. You will patrol the playing area, watching especially for cases of cheating and stealing. Offenders may be arrested and jailed for periods of one to five minutes. You should be particularly wary of the poor, as they are the most likely to cause trouble. Don't stand any nonsense!

WELFARE WORKERS

Your job is to assess and assist genuine cases of need. The money enclosed in this envelope is to be used for relief. Some of the citizens are very poor and in genuine distress. However, you must be on your guard against unscrupulous characters who may attempt to obtain money under false pretences. Make very careful enquiries of each applicant. Urge all applicants to try other ways of getting money (for example, work). Don't be too generous with your handouts — it only encourages laziness, and no more funds are available when you have used this money. It's a good idea to keep people waiting, just to show that you are not too soft a touch — after you have heard their applications, suggest that they come back in five minutes' time for your decision.

CLERGYMAN

The enclosed money is a special fund for poor relief. The fund may be built up by soliciting donations from wealthy citizens and business people. Don't be too quick to give handouts to the poor. True, some are in genuine need, but there are others who are out for whatever they can get. As far as possible, direct people to the welfare workers for financial help. Stress the importance of spiritual rather than material values. Remind people that "the love of money is the root of all evil", and that "man does not live by bread alone". Suggest that they put aside worldly cares and concentrate on higher things.

ORGANIZER OF THE POOR

Your job is to find out who are the genuinely poor people in this community, and to get them to work together for a better deal. You may work towards this goal in either a destructive or a constructive way. You may try to organize sit-ins, demonstrations, boycotts, or form a co-op or try group bargaining. Be wary of the police — they may not approve of your activities. In fact, it may be best if you keep your role a secret, at least from the police and welfare agencies.

NEWSPAPER REPORTER (if appointed)

Your job is to observe what happens in this community and to make a report at the end of the game. The enclosed money is an expense allowance. You may pay for stories, promise to give publicity to the poor (or to others), and follow up anything that looks like news. Take notes during the game, so that you can give an accurate report at the end. Watch especially for conflict, and for "human interest" stories.

* * * * * *

Set up the playing area. Shops may specialize, or all may carry the same lines. You will need a *church* for the clergyman, *offices* for the welfare workers and the newspaper reporter, and a *jail* for the police officers. No special territory will be assigned to the citizens — each one will have to find a spot for himself.

Action

1. Distribute the sealed envelopes, but ask the participants not to open them yet.

2. Explain that the main action of the game will involve those designated CITIZENS in constructing collages, with a thirty-minute time limit.

3. Say that materials for constructing the collages will be available from the shops. You may need to explain "collage" briefly. If necessary, explain the monetary system. (If you are using play money, there will not be much need for explanation. However, if you are using chips of different colours, explain their relative values.) Ask the SHOPKEEPERS to go to their shops now and open their sealed envelopes.

4. Mention that there is a police force to preserve law and order. POLICE OFFICERS should take up their positions at the jail and open their envelopes.

5. Point out that some citizens may find themselves in financial difficulties. If so, they may apply to the WELFARE WORKERS for relief. The welfare workers now go to their offices and open their envelopes.

6. Indicate the church, and talk about its presence as a source of strength and inspiration to the whole community. The CLERGYMAN should take up his position and open his envelope.

7. Say that a NEWSPAPER REPORTER will be observing what goes on in the community and nosing out the news. Indicate the newspaper office. The reporter takes up his position there and opens his envelope.

8. The remainder of the participants may now open their envelopes.

9. Check that all participants understand what they are to do.

10. Announce that the thirty-minute period is beginning. Note time. Player interaction begins. During the interaction period you (the game director) should be active also. Be pushy and insulting to the poor. Criticize their work and say they could do better.

11. Announce when the half-way mark has been reached; then when there are ten, five, three, two minutes, and one minute to go.

12. After thirty minutes, call time, and demand that all collages be displayed.

NOTE: It is possible that you will need to bring the game to an end before the thirty-minute period has elapsed. A certain amount of conflict is inevitable in a game of this kind, but if you feel that things are really getting out of hand, stop the game immediately and proceed with post-game discussion.

At the end of the game, ask the participants to abandon their roles and talk about the game experience. Questions such as these may be used to open up the issues:

Who ended with most money? Why?

What actually happened in the game? If you had a newspaper reporter he/she should report on his/her observations.

What kinds of pressures and frustrations did you (citizens) feel? How did you meet them?

How did the organizer of the poor fare?

What people in our society could be compared with the "poor" in the game?

What hope is there for the poor in our society? Who cares about them or helps them?

Does the church show out better in real life than it did in the game?

(If the game had to be stopped before the thirty-minute limit) What were the causes of the conflict? What would have happened if the game had continued? Are there similar conflicts in real life? What happens then?

CRISIS
in
the
CHURCH

A game by Pat Baker.

This game simulates a crisis in the local congregation, arising out of an action by youth group members.

The purposes of the simulation are

a) to experience inter-group conflict and to experiment with ways of resolving it,
b) to explore different understandings of the role of the church in society.

Number of players: Minimum of eight, plus game director. The players should be divided into groups as follows:

Local Church Authority, which you can call the Session, the Leaders' Meeting, the Parish Council, or whatever applies in your situation (up to twelve players)

Pastoral Committee (up to ten players)

Local Education Committee (up to ten players)

Youth Group (approximately one-fifth of total number of players)

Church Members (no limit)

With only eight players, forget about the category "church members" and assign two players to each of the other groups.

Materials
A copy of the Summary of Events for each player. (The description of the demonstration is deliberately vague. You can add topical details: what the protest is against, for example. If demonstrations are a dead issue in your community, some other form of public and controversial action may be substituted as the event which sparks off the crisis.)

A Group Briefing sheet for each group.

One copy of the Special Input for each group.

SUMMARY OF EVENTS
(copy to each player)

The following is a summary of the events which have led up to the present crisis. These are all generally known to members of the congregation.

SATURDAY

Most of the members of the Youth Group and a few adult members of the church take part in a protest demonstration involving about 2000 people. It ends in a violent confrontation with anti-protest forces. About fifty arrests are made, though none of the church people are arrested. Robert Brown, a member of the Youth Group, is interviewed by a TV reporter. He identifies himself as a member of the church and says that he is taking part in the demonstration because he is a Christian. He goes on to say that the Youth Group has been studying social and political issues and that the members are convinced that Christians must be involved in radical action to renew society.

SUNDAY

The Sunday paper gives front-page coverage to the violent confrontation. The Youth Group is not mentioned.

At the morning service the minister says that he has received telephone calls from several church members, expressing concern over the church's name being linked with radical action and violence. He makes a plea for understanding and Christian grace on the part of all concerned. The main point of his sermon is the Christian's obligation to stand firm in his convictions.

After the service a couple of influential church members are observed to ignore the minister's outstretched hand. They go off, apparently angry, without speaking to anyone.

MONDAY

The morning paper features an interview with the minister, under the heading "RADICAL REVEREND BACKS YOUTH PROTESTORS".

TUESDAY

The morning paper prints half a dozen letters commenting on various aspects of the demonstration. One of them criticizes the Youth Group's involvement in the demonstration and also comments on the minister's remarks as reported in Monday's paper.

An editorial in the same paper suggests that Communist influence was behind the demonstration.

WEDNESDAY

Overnight the front door of the church has been painted red. Painted on the wall are the words: "FOR COMMUNISTS ONLY".

Many more letters appear in the paper. They are mainly critical, but two commend the Youth Group's participation in the demonstration and the backing given by the minister. One of the critical letters is signed by a wealthy member of the church. He identifies himself as a member, but hints that he may withdraw his support if the church "continues to involve itself in matters which should not concern it".

News of the church-daubing hits the afternoon papers and the TV newscasts. It is reported in terms of "the price of radical action".

The Local Church Authority calls an emergency meeting for tonight to assess the situation. All church members are entitled to be present. Members of the Pastoral Committee, the Local Education Committee, and the Youth Group are particularly asked to attend. It is generally anticipated that the Youth Group will be hauled over the coals. Only members of the Local Church Authority are entitled to vote at the meeting. Tomorrow night there will be a meeting of the entire congregation to discuss the matter and to decide where the church goes from here. All members will be entitled to vote at that meeting.

GROUP BRIEFINGS
(copy of the appropriate sheet to each group)

WEDNESDAY

You are the **Local Church Authority.** You are meeting to discuss the crisis that has arisen in the church following the Youth Group's participation in the demonstration last weekend. You have called an emergency meeting for tonight. All church members may attend, but you have specially asked that members of the Pastoral Committee, the Local Education Committee, and the Youth Group be present. You have fifteen minutes to prepare an agenda for the meeting and to plan strategy. You will need to appoint a chairman to preside at the meeting. You are responsible for the general functioning of the church and all its organizations. Your main concern is for the good of the church as a whole. Three members of the Local Church Authority are parents of youth group members.

In addition to what is known to all members of the congregation, you have the following information:

1. You have received a carbon copy of a letter sent to the minister by the Youth Group Committee, thanking him for his support over the demonstration.

2. Several important people in the community (not members of this church) have commented to Authority members about the situation. They have been critical, except for one who was "glad to see the church getting involved in important issues for a change".

3. Two church members with large pledges have threatened to withdraw their support unless the Youth Group is disciplined.

4. Rumour: Some other members are considering cancelling their pledges/transferring their membership elsewhere.

5. Rumour: It was a member of the Youth Group who tipped off the TV people about the church-daubing this morning.

*　*　*　*　*　*

WEDNESDAY

You are the **Pastoral Committee.** You are meeting to discuss the crisis that has arisen in the church following the Youth Group's participation in the demonstration last weekend. An emergency meeting of the Local Church Authority has been called for tonight and you have been asked to attend. You are responsible for assisting the minister in the pastoral oversight of the whole congregation. You also feel a responsibility to function as a support group to the minister. Choose one member of the group to play the role of the minister, the Rev. William Gray. You have fifteen minutes in which to discuss the situation and to plan strategy for tonight's meeting. One member of the committee is the parent of a Youth Group member who was involved in the demonstration.

In addition to what is known to all members of the congregation, you have the following information:

1. The minister has received many telephone calls and letters from both church members and others, commenting on the situation. About half have been critical, expressing alarm at the way in which the church's name has been linked with the protest movement.

2. The minister has received a letter from the Youth Group committee, thanking him for his support over the demonstration, and stating that they are sending a carbon copy to the Local Church Authority.

3. The minister's wife has had to deal with several anonymous, abusive 'phone calls. She is having trouble sleeping at night.

4. Several church members are putting pressure on the minister to discipline the Youth Group and to disown the stand attributed to him in Monday morning's paper.

5. The report of the interview in Monday's paper is substantially correct, but the minister regrets the headline, which was used without his prior knowledge.

6. Three people have asked to have their names removed from the church membership rolls.

*　*　*　*　*　*

WEDNESDAY

You are the **Local Education Committee.** You are meeting to discuss the crisis that has arisen in the church following the Youth Group's participation in the demonstration last weekend. An emergency meeting of the Local Church Authority has been called for tonight and you have been asked to attend. You are responsible for the planning and oversight of the church's total educational programme. Since the Youth Group's participation in the demonstration apparently stems from its study programme, you may come under fire at the meeting. You have fifteen minutes in which to discuss the situation and to plan strategy for tonight's meeting. Two members of the committee are parents of Youth Group members who took part in the demonstration. One member of the committee was also involved in the demonstration. Assign this role to a member of the group.

In addition to what is known to all members of the congregation, you have the following information:

1. One member of your committee also took part in the demonstration and is fully in agreement with the stand taken by the young people.

2. Rumour: At least two wealthy and influential church members have threatened to cancel their pledges.

3. The father of one of the girls in the Youth Group has expressed concern at their study of social and political issues. He demands that this study programme be terminated and that a course of Bible study replace it. He claims to have the support of "at least half the parents of Youth Group members".

4. Robert Brown has told one of your members that the young people are convinced that they are in the right in this matter, and that they will stand by all that they and the minister have said.

* * * * * *

WEDNESDAY
You are the **Youth Group.** You are meeting to discuss the crisis that has arisen in the church following your participation in the demonstration last weekend. An emergency meeting of the Local Church Authority has been called for tonight and you have been asked to attend. You anticipate fireworks. You have fifteen minutes in which to discuss the situation and to plan strategy for tonight's meeting. You expect to be asked to justify the action taken by the young people last Saturday and the statement made by Robert Brown. One member of the group should play the role of Robert Brown.

In addition to what is known to all members of the congregation, you have the following information:

1. The Youth Group committee has sent a letter to the minister, thanking him for his support in this matter. A carbon copy has been sent to the Local Church Authority.

2. One of the TV channels wants to feature the church in a special documentary programme which will explain how and why the Youth Group has become involved in radical action.

The TV people made the approach through Robert Brown, who suggested that they contact the minister.

3. Robert Brown has received several anonymous 'phone calls along the lines that the Lord will punish him for his blasphemy and wickedness.

4. Rumour: The Local Education Committee is going to stop all youth activities except for a Bible study programme.

5. One member of the Local Education Committee also took part in the demonstration. You believe he/she is in full agreement with your stand and will support you at the meeting.

* * * * * *

WEDNESDAY
You are **Church Members.** You are meeting to discuss the crisis that has arisen in the church following the Youth Group's participation in the demonstration last weekend. An emergency meeting of the Local Church Authority has been called for tonight. As church members you are entitled to attend the meeting, but not to vote. Some of you are parents of Youth Group members. Some your-selves took part in the demonstration. You have fifteen minutes in which to discuss the situation in preparation for tonight's meeting.

In addition to what is generally known about the situation, the following rumours are circulating:

1. The Local Church Authority is going to ask for the minister's resignation unless he makes a public statement disowning the stand attributed to him in Monday morning's paper.

2. The minister's wife is on the verge of a nervous breakdown.

3. Several families have left the church because of what has happened.

4. The Youth Group is going to be closed down.

5. One of the richest members has cancelled his pledge.

6. There has been a threat to burn down the church.

* * * * * *

CHANNEL X

By Special Messenger

The Reverend William Gray,
Community Church,
Greenville.

Dear Mr. Gray,

We were in contact earlier today with Robert Brown, a member of your Youth Group. Robert, of course, is known to us through his participation in the protest demonstration last Saturday. He suggested that we get in touch with you.

In line with our policy of getting behind the news to let the public know what is really happening in our community, we would like to feature your church - and especially its young people - in a thirty-minute documentary entitled "Radical Religion".

We will want coverage of the normal Sunday functions of the church, plus interviews with you, the young people who were involved in the demonstration, and the various officers and leaders of the church. This could be shot this coming weekend: key interviews on Saturday, worship and other activities on Sunday morning together with some man-in-the-pew comments, with a view to using it on Monday night.

We need an immediate reply, so that we can get things rolling. (You will appreciate our haste: your church is news now. In a couple of weeks, the world may have forgotten all about you.)

Channel X will, of course, be making a donation to your church's funds, in appreciation of your anticipated cooperation.

Sincerely yours,

Henry Lawson

Henry Lawson,
Documentary Programmes.

SPECIAL INPUT
(copy for each group in Step 4)

Timetable

1. Introduction (10 minutes)

2. Group Meetings (15 minutes)

3. Meeting of Local Church Authority (20 minutes)

4. (Special Input)

5. Group Meetings (15 minutes)

6. Congregational Meeting (30 minutes)

7. Evaluation (30 minutes)

Total playing time: 2 hours

Action

1. The game director outlines the purpose of the simulation. Each player receives a copy of the Summary of Events, which is then examined. The game director outlines the timetable, *omitting any mention of the Special Input which follows the meeting of the Local Church Authority.*

The players are divided into groups. No specific roles are assigned by the game director, but the Local Church Authority is asked to appoint a chairman, and the Pastoral Committee should choose one of its members to play the role of the minister, the Rev. William Gray. (The Authority chairman will preside at the meeting of the Local Church Authority, and the minister at the Congregational Meeting.) The Youth Group should choose someone to play the role of Robert Brown, and the Local Education Committee the member who took part in the demonstration.

Each group moves to its meeting area. The Group Briefing sheets are distributed. (If more than twelve people are in the Church Members group, this group should be divided for easier discussion. In this case, different rumours or combinations of rumours could be given to each sub-group.) When all groups have received their Briefing Sheets, announce the beginning of the Group Meeting period.

2. Group Meetings for fifteen minutes. During this time the groups discuss the crisis and decide on strategy for the meeting of the Local Church Auth-

ority. In addition to discussing the situation, the Local Church Authority draws up the agenda for the meeting.

3. The groups come together for the Local Church Authority meeting. The chairman presides. Anyone is permitted to speak, but only the members of the Local Church Authority may vote on any matter.

At the close of the meeting (after 20 minutes) the game director announces that the groups have a further fifteen minutes to prepare for the Congregational Meeting. Unless other arrangements have been made at the present meeting, the Pastoral Committee should draw up the agenda for the Congregational Meeting.

4. As soon as the groups have returned to their meeting areas the Special Input (letter from Channel X) is given to each group.

5. Group Meetings for fifteen minutes. During this time the groups discuss their strategy for the Congregational Meeting in the light of developments at the meeting of the Local Church Authority and taking into account the new information contained in the Special Input.

6. Congregational Meeting, with the minister presiding. All members are permitted to speak, and to vote. Time limit: 30 minutes.

7. The whole group looks back over the exercise and relates the simulation to its own situation. Use questions like these:

> What decisions were made?
> How did people feel at particular points?
> What groups found themselves in conflict with other groups?
> What points were matters of conflict?
> What could have happened to change the outcome?
> What usually happens when there is conflict in a church?
> What kinds of issues are likely to cause conflict?
> How can conflicts be resolved?
> Ought the church to keep out of conflict situations?

CRYSTAL PISTOL

Reprinted from YOUTH MINISTRY TRAINING KIT. Copyright © 1970 by The Seabury Press, Inc., New York. Used by permission.

Allow two to three hours for this exercise.

It is the leader's task to transform the facilities in your meeting place into the town of Fenton, and to assign parts and transform the participants into the people of Fenton with all the dynamics that are present in the situation.

Then you simply let the action spin out. Whatever happens, happens. Do not try to influence the outcome in any way. Do not worry about how people behave or what they say.

You will need:

1. Locations and signs for the meeting places:
    - The Crystal Pistol
    - The Cattleman
    - The Brass Ring
    - Police Headquarters

2. A copy of the situation for each participant.

3. To assign the names of participants to parts before the plenary session for the simulation. If you have more adults than the simulation calls for, invent names for them and add them as interested people to the meetings at "The Crystal Pistol" or "The Cattleman". If you have too few adults, delete (1) Miss Ida Curtis; (2) Mr. Earl Shaffer. (If necessary, you might also delete some of the young people's roles.)

4. To prepare a name tag with each person's simulation name in large letters. Keep the name tags in order. Be sure to provide pins.

Time and place: Friday afternoon in Fenton (which you may imagine as a town in your state or province).

The situation

"The Crystal Pistol" is a centre for teenagers that is located in the main street of Fenton. It was started about a year ago, mainly through the efforts of Donald Phelps, the young minister of the Presbyterian Church. Mr. Phelps saw that there were a number of young people who really had no place to gather on weekends. He got in touch with four adults from different churches in Fenton: Mr. and Mrs. Samuels, Joe Curry, and Edith Pauls; and they persuaded others to donate enough money to rent a shop the high school kids could convert into a meeting place.

The "Pistol" is now a going concern. On weekends large numbers of young people show up there to sit around and talk, to listen to music, to read their own poetry, and to exhibit their own art. The adults have maintained their interest and have enlisted the help of half a dozen other adults. They come to the "Pistol" to serve coffee or hot chocolate or soft drinks and talk with the teenagers.

There are two fancy restaurants in the same block as the "Pistol" in Bedford Street. "The Cattleman" is owned by Mr. Fournier and "Sherman's" is owned by Mrs. Sherman. Both these business people are very much concerned about the "Pistol". Groups of teenagers gather on the footpath along Bedford Street. They go in and out of the "Pistol", but there are always clusters of young people with long hair and old jeans loitering in groups of five or six at various places outside.

The customers who come to eat at "The Cattleman" or at "Sherman's" are constantly complaining about the young people on the street. The adults don't like the idea of "having to fight their way through that mob of delinquents outside". Mr. Fournier and Mrs. Sherman are becoming painfully conscious that their customers are going to the other side of the town on weekends. The local police chief, Sergeant Phil Dawson, is aware of the problem. He has assured the restaurant owners that if he receives a complaint, he will send police officers to "deal with the situation".

Mr. Phelps and the other adult workers at "The Crystal Pistol" know that the restaurant owners are concerned, and they have spoken to the teenagers about the situation. The kids feel they have a perfect right to stand wherever they want to on the public streets, and they resent the restaurant owners' attitude.

The Restaurant Owners' Association has called a meeting at 2.00 p.m. "to come to a decision about our policy towards the teenage situation on the street". The Association has announced that at 2.30 they will send word to Sergeant Dawson to give him their decision as to whether they will need police assistance tonight.

At 1.45 p.m. today the adult workers and the Teenage Advisory Council of the "Pistol" are coming together for an emergency meeting.

A third group is also planning to meet at 1.00 p.m. These are high school young people who feel that the adult workers at the "Pistol" probably won't stand up for the kids' rights. Some of these young people, led by Tony DeNucci, a senior student at Fenton High School, hope to convince the others that if the police are called in, the high school students should make a real demonstration. Others in the group feel that if it comes to resisting the police, it would be better to "go along with whatever's decided".

Meeting at "The Crystal Pistol" at 1.45 p.m.

THE REV. DONALD PHELPS
Minister of the Presbyterian Church, organizer and chairman of the Advisory Board of "The Crystal Pistol".

MR. JOHN SAMUELS
Member of St. Paul's Anglican Church; a prominent businessman in Fenton and a supporter of "The Crystal Pistol", both financially and as a volunteer worker.

MRS. NANCY SAMUELS
Wife of John Samuels; a socially conscious woman who wants "something for the kids", but tries to avoid controversy; serves coffee and hot chocolate at "The Crystal Pistol".

JOE CURRY

A truck driver who comes to the "Pistol" after work on weekends because he likes the kids; not much education, but willing to do anything to help out; doesn't belong to any church, but sometimes goes to the Church of Christ "because my mother belonged there".

EDITH PAULS

A girl who has come back to her home town to teach in the primary school. She is a member of St. Boniface Roman Catholic Church. Many of the young people are also Roman Catholic and are friends of Edith's young sister Ruth.

SHIRLEY COMBS	
ROGER DONELIAN	Members of
GINGER HASTIE	"The Crystal
RUSSELL MAY	Pistol"
RUTH PAULS (Edith's sister)	Teenage
JULIE STANTON	Advisory
BILL WHITAKER	Council
BOB YOUNG	

MRS. JOAN CARTER

A wealthy lady who serves as a volunteer director of the Mayor's Fund (a local charity). The Mayor has sent her to the meeting at the "Pistol". Mr. Phelps has not met her nor is he aware that she is coming to the meeting. The Mayor has urged her "to try to get those people to see what's best for this town and its image throughout the state".

DARLENE SAUNDERS

A newspaper reporter who has written a series of articles on teenage problems and supports the restaurant owners in their feeling that "this nuisance has to be dealt with". Mr. Phelps has asked her to come to the "Pistol" to hear their side of the story.

Meeting at "The Cattleman" with the Restaurant Owners' Association at 2.00 p.m.

MR. RICHARD FOURNIER

Owner of "The Cattleman" restaurant; treasurer of St. Paul's Anglican Church; member of the Restaurant Owners' Association.

MRS. BERTHA SHERMAN

Owner of "Sherman's" restaurant; secretary of the Restaurant Owners' Association.

MISS IDA CURTIS

Member of the Restaurant Owners' Association; owner of the "Delmonico Restaurant" on the other side of town.

MR. RALPH POWERS

President of the Restaurant Owners' Association; owner of the large "Fenton Club", which serves only the very wealthy people of the area; senior warden of St. Paul's Anglican Church.

MR. WALLACE BROWN

Co-owner of the "Brass Ring Coffee Lounge". Located a block east of Bedford Street in Fourth Street, it is a place where young people are likely to hang out when "The Crystal Pistol" isn't open; member of the Restaurant Owners' Association.

MR. EARL SHAFFER

Co-owner of the "Brass Ring Coffee Lounge"; member of the Restaurant Owners' Association.

FREDDY MILES

Owner of "The Merry-Go-Round" newspaper and tobacco shop, which serves most of the men in Fenton. Freddy hears a lot of complaints from adults who feel that the police ought to put a stop to teenagers hanging around Bedford Street on Friday and Saturday evenings. A good friend of Mr. Fournier, Freddy has been invited to the meeting of the Restaurant Owners' Association.

MRS. GLADYS KAUFFMAN

Senior mistress at Fenton High School; asked by the restaurant owners to come to the R.O.A. meeting "to clarify the school's policy on the activities of students outside school time".

THE REV. WILLIAM STACY

Rector of St. Paul's Anglican Church. Mr. Powers, president of R.O.A., is senior warden of St. Paul's, a very conservative parish that carries on quite traditional programmes for young people. Mr. Powers has asked Father Stacy to talk to the members of the Restaurant Owners' Association about "The Crystal Pistol" from the church's point of view.

At the police station

SERGEANT PHILIP DAWSON
Officer in charge.

Circulating among the meetings

KATHY NICHOLS

Radio news commentator for the local station; Kathy is interested in talking to as many of the people involved in the situation as possible for a special feature she is preparing for her evening broadcast. Whatever decision is reached, Kathy wants to help her listeners understand how the whole thing started.

Meeting at the "Brass Ring Coffee Lounge"

A group of teenagers who sometimes come to "The Crystal Pistol". Some are friends of Tony DeNucci; some know him slightly. The word that "something's brewing" has brought all of them to the "Brass Ring" this afternoon.

TONY DE NUCCI

A senior high school student; he has a reputation with adults of being "hard to handle". Tony and some of the others want to talk about "what's going to happen tonight when the cops arrive".

JOYCE DAVIS
JOE WENDELL
DICK SINCLAIR
JOHN COHEN
DOUG PALMER
DON EDWARDS
SAM ULMER
TERRY WESTCOTT (Joe Wendells's girlfriend)
PEG FINE
PENNY LARSON
ELSA STEIN
MISSY COLLINS
JANICE VAUGHN
LISA FOSTER
DEBBY SHUTE
GINNY HELD
CHRIST BERNHARDT.
SUE HEMINGWAY

A suggested procedure

* Place a chair for each participant in a large circle, with two chairs in the centre of the circle.

* Distribute copies of the description of the situation and have it read aloud.

* Ask participants to come — one at a time, beginning with the person you have chosen to be the Rev. Donald Phelps — to the other chair in the centre of the circle. Give the participant his name tag, say his name clearly, and explain his part as it is described in the role descriptions given above. Be sure everyone can hear.

* To speed up the process, the members of the Teenage Advisory Council may be given name tags and parts as a group. They may sit on the floor in the centre of the circle as you give each his name tag and say his name for the total group.

* The same procedure may be followed for Tony DeNucci and his friends. Explain that the Advisory Council of "The Crystal Pistol", the Restaurant Owners' Association, or the group of high school students may send a representative or representatives to the other groups when there is a request or a decision to communicate, or when a group has questions to ask the others.

* Announce the meeting places and let the action begin.

* As leader, circulate among the groups and listen. Make your decision to cut the action while interest is still high. There is a built-in time for the decision of the Restaurant Owners' Association, but action may well go on until the responses of the other groups have been made.

* When you announce that the simulation is over, ask the total group to return to the original circle. The de-roling process is sometimes quite difficult for people who have built up strong emotional investments in what has happened. You can help by encouraging and reminding people to refer to their character in the third person: "Joyce did such-and-such", rather than "I did such-and-such". Questions that are helpful in de-roling are:

> What did he try to do or be?
> What helped him to do or be that?
> What worked against him?

* After the individuals have had a chance to reflect on their own parts in the situation, collect the simulation name tags.

* See if the group can identify and give examples of some of the forces and factors present in the situation. Move on to consider what happens in situations of conflict between people. What can we do as individuals in such situations? What can we do as the church?

THE GAP

A game by Marelle Harrison.

Aims

To experience the inability of people in unskilled and semi-skilled jobs to rise out of their situation, and the increasing gap that comes between them and the traders and professional people in the community.

To apply this to the Aboriginal community.

To experience the effect that role expectations of job titles (categories) have on the way persons treat each other in economic transactions.

To apply these learnings to our own community.

Preparation for the game

1. Obtain 100 counters of any colour or colours. They are all worth the same amount.

2. Prepare a chart containing instructions as below:

- Spend a period of time trading the goods you have to offer or the labour you can give at the highest possible price.
- Try to obtain the products/services you need at the lowest possible price.

3. Prepare a set of cards listing products and needs for each job, as below:

Bark Painters — you have paintings to sell; you need food, medical help, clothing, legal advice, housing.

Horse Riders — you can drove cattle or sheep, mend fences; you need food, clothing, housing, medical services, legal aid.

Labourers — you can carry bricks, mix cement, dig drains, do gardening, wash floors; you need food, medical and legal aid, clothing, housing.

Shop Keepers — you have food and clothing to sell; you need people to work in and clean the shop, deliver parcels, shift stock, medical and legal advice, housing.

Builders — you have timber and building materials, and can build houses; you need labourers and skilled tradesmen, food, clothing, medical and legal advice, and land.

Lawyers — you can give legal advice; you need food, clothing, medical advice, housing, opportunities to invest money.

Farmers — you have land, cattle and sheep, homestead; you need labour to round up animals, mend fences, clean house, and clothing, medical and legal advice, more land.

Doctors — you can give medical advice; you need food, clothing, legal advice, cleaning services, gardening services, housing, and opportunities to invest money.

4. Distribute the chips in the following proportions to the eight players or teams:

Bark painters — 4; horse riders — 7; labourers — 6; builders — 15; shop keepers — 15; farmers — 15; lawyers — 18; doctors — 18.

5. At the end of the trading period, have each team add up their chips and compare gains or losses in terms of what they started with.

6. Discuss the implications of the game for the "upward social and economic mobility" of Aborigines in Australia today.

NOTE: The game is easily adapted for New Zealand use by changing some of the roles. You could include the following categories:

Weavers — you have kilts, head bands, mats, baskets and taniko weaving to sell; you need food, clothing, medical and legal aid, housing.

Carvers — you have carved figures, canoes and panels to sell; you need food, clothing, medical and legal aid, housing.

Singers and dancers — you can perform hakas and poi dances and sing Maori songs; you need food, clothing, medical and legal aid, housing.

Immigrants

This description is from information provided by Bryan Worsnop.

A game was devised for the 1972 Methodist Youth Fellowship Congress, held at Ivanhoe, Victoria. Delegates knew that the theme of the Congress was to be "Migration". This is how the action went when they arrived at Ivanhoe —

1. **"Welcome"**. The entrance from the street led to the hall. The half of the hall which the delegates entered was designated the "welcome area". The other half was partitioned off. Delegates had to stand around for several minutes (no chairs provided) until they were called through the partition.

2. **Waiting.** On the other side of the partition delegates found themselves in the "waiting room", where they were told to remain until called to the "interview area". Seats were provided in the waiting room, but no magazines or other distractions from boredom. The interview area was hidden by screens.

3. **Interview 1.** One by one the delegates were called to the interview area. This was divided into small cubicles, each with a desk, two interviewers, and a chair for the delegate. Each delegate was asked his name, was checked off the list, issued with a name tag, and sent to another waiting area.

4. **Interview 2.** The second waiting area had a row of chairs, and a table in one corner. After waiting for a while, the delegate was called into a second interview room, handed a questionnaire, and told to fill it in at the table in the waiting room. When called back to the interview room, he handed over the questionnaire and was immediately referred to yet another waiting area.

5. **Interview 3.** After waiting for a while, delegates in turn were called into a very dimly lit interview room, again with two interviewers seated behind a desk, and a chair for the delegate. The interviewers rattled off questions in a foreign language and did not appear to understand English. After the interview, the delegate was told (in English, by someone else) where to go next.

6. **Interview 4.** The next stop was a large room with the interview area in full view of the waiting room. In the waiting room each person was given a form (printed in Italian) to fill in. Pens and pencils were provided. The completed form was to be handed to the interviewers, who spent most of the evening sending them back to be filled in "properly". (Those done in ink had to be re-done in pencil, and vice versa.) When the interviewer was satisfied, the delegate was handed a Congress kit and sent to the next interview room.

7. **Interview 5.** This interview area was manned by only one person and it was here that the delegate was given instructions about his group placement for the weekend. He also heard the good news that, if he would care to wait a little while in the next room, he would be able to watch a film.

8. **Film.** When a group of about twenty people had built up, they were led to another room where the film was shown — with Italian commentary and no English sub-titles. (Several different films were used during the course of the evening.) By this time the delegates were beginning to think it would never end.

9. **Discussion.** A lot of bewildered people staggered out of the film into a large room where they found chairs, tables, biscuits and coffee. Here they discussed the game experience.

This simulation was the introduction to a series of contacts with migrant groups through the course of the weekend Congress.

A variation of this game, used at a migrant appreciation day at Brunswick, Victoria, was described in *Learning Exchange,* No. 7. An additional feature was the "passport" which was issued at the first interview. The front page of the passport had space for each interviewer to sign his name and place a stamp. These signatures had to be obtained in a specific order, but it was not pointed out to the participants that the signatures and stamps were required at all. Some of the interviewers purposely did not sign unless asked, hence the "migrant" had to be sent back by the next interviewer to correct the omission.

THE MILK RUN

A game by Jack Anderson.

Objectives

Groups and individuals find that decision-making is a most difficult task to learn. Simply talking about how decisions are made is usually futile. Learning only *really* takes place as individuals and/or groups directly participate in the process of decision-making.

The objective of "Milk Run" is to enable groups and individuals within groups to "play" with the decision-making process and then evaluate how the dynamics which come into play might be helpful in "for-real" decision-making. The after game debriefing is as important as the game itself.

Setting

The Grateful Guernsey Milk Company employs a staff of five truck drivers to deliver its products to urban, suburban, and rural Drinkstown. Every so often the company purchases a new truck to exchange for an old one, and the route foreman always has a difficult problem deciding which of the drivers should have the new truck. In the past, there have been hard feelings because each driver seems to think he or she is entitled to the new truck.

It's most difficult to find a fair way of handling truck distribution. And no matter how fair it seems to the foreman, someone always feels "wronged". It's that time again and the foreman, Arthur, has called a staff meeting to discuss who the drivers think the new Toyota truck should be given to.

Here is the data on the route men:

SID (aged 62) — 18 years with G.G. Milk Co., has a 2-year-old Ford truck.

CHARLIE (57) — 12 years with G.G. Milk Co., has a 5-year-old Bedford truck.

TOM (49) — 11 years with G.G. Milk Co., has a 4-year-old Ford truck.

FRANK (35) — 6 years with G.G. Milk Co., has a 3-year-old Ford truck.

MELVA (a 34-year-old lady) — 4 years with the G.G. Milk Co., has a 5-year-old Bedford.

All of the drivers do either urban or suburban driving, making fairly short trips, except for Tom and Frank who have rural routes.

In order to handle the problem Arthur, the foreman, has put the decision in the hands of the drivers themselves. The decision must be acceptable to *all* members of the truck crew.

To help the drivers get into character

SID: When the new Toyota truck becomes available, you think you should have it because you have most seniority and don't like your present truck. Your own car is a Toyota, and you did a test run in a Toyota truck when the company first thought of buying one.

CHARLIE: You feel you deserve a new truck. Your present truck is old, and since the senior man has a fairly new truck, you should get the next one. You have taken excellent care of your present Bedford truck and have kept it looking new. A driver deserves to be rewarded if he treats a company truck like his own.

TOM: You have to do more driving than most of the other men because yours is a rural route. You have a fairly old truck and feel you should have the new one because you do so much driving.

FRANK: The heater in your present truck is inadequate. Since Melva backed into the door of your truck, it has never been repaired to fit right. The door lets in too much cold air, and you attribute your frequent colds to this. You have missed a good deal of work due to sickness and the foreman has warned you that any more time off might cost you your job. You want a warm truck since you also have a rural route. As long as it has good tyres, brakes, and is comfortable you don't care about its make or age.

MELVA: You have the poorest truck in the crew. It is five years old, and before you got it, it had been in a bad wreck. It has never been good and you've put up with it for three years. It's about time someone showed you some courtesy, and a new truck would be the best way possible. You have a good accident record. The only accident you had was when you sprung the door on Frank's truck when he opened it as you backed away from the loading dock. You hope the new truck is a Ford since you prefer driving one. You're constantly angered at the way the other drivers treat you because you get no respect.

Suggestions for playing "Milk Run"

1. Choose Arthur, the foreman (who attempts to remain neutral throughout the process), Sid, Charlie, Tom, Frank, and Melva.

2. Allow them to see *only* what pertains to the development of their own character.

3. Choose six observers to study the dynamics of the group interaction.

4. Introduce other ad lib factors as you see fit. For example: Melva announces toward the end of the process that she is pregnant and will be leaving in thirty days, and that a new man has already been hired and the boss promised him a truck no more than two years old. OR, Sid has decided that if he does not get the new truck he will retire, and the foreman is afraid that if Sid retires the boss will decide against purchasing a new truck. OR dream up your own ways of complicating things. You might even pre-plan an inflamatory situation where two of the men almost come to blows.

After-game debriefing

1. Did you come to an acceptable decision?

2. What factors helped you come to that decision?

3. What factors hindered you from making the decision?

4. What were the feelings of the crew at different times in the game?

5. What did the observers note as to those dynamics at play in the process?

6. How can the game help us look at decision-making in our group? In our own lives?

7. If the observers were playing in place of those who did play, whom would they choose to be and what would they do differently?

8. Is the process different in group decision-making than in individual decision-making?

9. How do we usually make decisions in our group? Who makes the final decision?

Please evaluate

The designer of this game would like your comments after you have played it. Please send to:

Jack N. Anderson,
Director of Religious Education
Office of the Post Chaplain
Building 41
Fort McPherson, Georgia 30330, U.S.A.

PROJECT ECONOMY

Report of a summer camp simulation devised by the Rev. Albert Zehr, of Baden, Ontario, Canada. Reprinted from SPECTRUM/International Journal of Religious Education, May/June 1970 issue. Used by permission.

When questioned about it later, about half the population admitted, "I defrauded either other people or the government".

The poor were frustrated, despondent, suspicious of one another. The rich overcharged everyone for everything so that they could pay the high taxes and still make a profit. They complained about the difficulties of being and staying rich; some felt guilty; no one, though, gave his wealth away. Middle-class people who wanted to make a little extra money took jobs from the poor who could not afford to work for so little money.

Inflation got so out of hand that the price of a hot dog went up to $50, and the poor went without meals.

Almost like real life, all this actually occurred among a group of 23 Mennonite youth at a summer camp near Hamburg, Ontario, in Canada. They were involved in a simulation experience called "Project Economy", an experiment its instigator, Rev. Albert Zehr, hoped might help the participants "experience the dynamics at work between the rich and the poor and the emotions and feelings rampant when one is caught in the rat-race of today's economic system".

c

Getting started

The participants arrived on a Thursday evening and immediately set about playing games of Monopoly. There were four players in each game and the game ended when one of the players went bankrupt. The money, or lack of it, remaining to each player became his cash assets for the continuing experiment. It was agreed that anything acceptable in present-day society would be acceptable in this simulated economy.

The government (Mr. Zehr) auctioned off the facilities of the camp. Meals, sleeping blankets, washrooms, the swimming pool, pool table, and even the toilets were bought by purchasers with an eye to making a profit from resale or rental. The poor waited patiently in hopes of getting work so that they might afford at least a sleeping blanket for the first night.

Government action

During the course of the experiment moves by the government became necessary to bring reality into the situation. Taxes were imposed on income, property, luxuries, and gifts. Tax collecting jobs were auctioned off by sealed bids. "Secret agents" kept an eye out for any irregularities in tax collection or money transactions of any kind. The rich groaned and raised prices. The poor moaned and often did without.

Since many of the "citizens" began to spend their money with an eye to having it last just until the end of the experiment, it was necessary to create some kind of incentive to get and keep money. The offer of $1.00 in actual money for every $1,000 held by a participant at the end of the experiment worked effectively to provide a profit-making drive.

Effects

A number of phenomena common to the outside world developed in the course of the experiment. Some discontents "rioted" against the especially greedy owner of the ping pong table and dismantled the table. One exceptionally creative businesswoman made a contract with the government to supply the camp house with "window holder openers". She then in turn offered different parts of the job to sub-contractors. This helped to stimulate the economy.

However, on Saturday it became obvious that high taxes were draining the economy and the poor were not getting enough work. The government instituted a "Government Make Work Project", offering $50 each time a picnic table was carried around the lake. While some worked avidly at this project, others showed considerable hostility towards the "coolies" and "peasants" who would stoop to such demeaning labour. When the workers discovered a farm trailer and began to haul several tables at a time in it, they found to their chagrin that the government owned the trailer and would charge $20 rental for it each time around.

Public indignation about one swindler and tax-evader resulted in his getting a sentence of four hours of solitary confinement. Released after three hours ("for good behaviour"), he faced the problems of an ex-convict.

Evaluation

The experiment ended on Sunday morning, then several hours were spent evaluating it. All but three of the participants thought it had been a valuable experience. Several noted that they had got sick of the money obsession. One youth told an adult later, "It makes you feel low-down and ugly after you sneak some leftovers from someone else's plate. It made me feel like a dog."

According to Mr. Zehr, a simulation experience should so closely parallel an actual situation that many of the effects of the real situation will be experienced, and experienced in a much shorter time than the real experience might take. Most of all it should teach the participant what another person in a real life situation is experiencing.

In the evaluation of the experiment many felt that a larger group, up to fifty people, might be preferable. Mr. Zehr also feels that from three days to a week are necessary for a really effective experience. Considerable value might also be gained, he suggests, if the evaluation brings Christian values and their implications to bear on what has occurred.

FAMILY CHARADES

Materials

Packs of A, B, and C cards (see page 36). A bottle that spins (e.g., Pepsi or Coke). A score sheet and something to write with.

Goal

To get the greatest number of points at the end of the time. Points are gained by portraying roles and emotions so well that the other players guess them.

Preparation

Shuffle each pack of cards and have them ready on hand.

Have everyone sit around in a circle. Place the bottle on its side in the middle.

Procedure

1. The leader spins the bottle very hard, once. The person it points to is "A". He takes a role card from Pack A.

2. The leader spins the bottle again (or "A" spins it). The person it points to is "B". He takes a role card from Pack B.

3. Either "A" or "B" draws an emotion card from Pack C. He must portray that emotion to (in relation to) the other person. He may show the C card to the other, who must decide on and portray an appropriate response. The acting out will be done without the use of words. The two are members of one family, therefore, two sons are brothers, etc.

4. The other players try to guess —
a) A's role
b) B's role
c) the emotion on the C card
d) the emotion portrayed by the other person.

Scoring

"A" gets one point if his role is guessed correctly.

"B" gets one point is his role is guessed correctly.

Each gets one point if the emotion he portrays is guessed correctly.

Therefore, four possible points may be won in each round.

End game

Call time when attention lags, or after a predetermined time has passed. Total the individual scores.

Discuss

Talk about the emotions portrayed. Does your family feel these things about each other? Compare these human feelings with the feelings God must have Or any other appropriate discussion for your particular goal.

Adapt to your own purpose

Change packs A and B to any roles you want to emphasize. They are now designed to give various combinations of mother/father/son/daughter, with more chance of parent/child than child/child and no chance of parent/parent.

Eliminate the packs A and B and just use two roles: A is automatically parent, B is child. Or designate other roles as needed.

More negative emotions can be added to pack C.

Use a different method of selecting role players. Spinning the bottle is fun, but the bottle can be easily manipulated by the spinner. Some other kind of spinning device could be used. Or, to make sure that everyone gets an equal number of opportunities to role play (and therefore, to score), write the participants' names on slips of paper and draw two each round. The used slips are not replaced until everyone has had a turn.

Evaluation

This game worked well with youngsters of primary school age by letting A and B prepare for a minute or two in another corner while the rest of the group sang a song. The kids did well at portraying and guessing emotions, but found communicating roles more difficult.

Preparing the packs of cards

Since three packs are required, you could use three different colours. Otherwise, mark the backs of the cards clearly with a large A, B, or C. About 2" x 1" (5cm x 2.5cm) is usually a convenient size.

PACK A

Prepare an even number of cards for this pack. On half of them, write "son" and on the other half, "daughter". It doesn't matter exactly how many cards you have, though there should be at least half a dozen each of "son" and "daughter" cards.

PACK B

One-third of the cards in this pack should be marked "mother", one-third "father", one-sixth "son", and one-sixth, "daughter". That is, if you have a set of 30 cards, there should be 10 "mothers", 10 "fathers", 5 "sons", and 5 "daughters".

PACK C

The content of this pack is flexible, but each emotion ought to appear on at least two cards. The age group with which you are planning to use the game should be taken into consideration, as some of the more complex emotions may be too difficult for young players. Here are some suggestions:

gladness	pride	love
sadness	irritation	anger
grief	jealousy	guilt
joy	pleasure	hopefulness
admiration	sulkiness	disappointment

PAY-OFF

Cooperation

A game by Mary-Ruth Marshall.

The purpose of Pay-Off is to dramatize the merits of collaboration and cooperation as opposed to individual competition in any form of personal relationships. It deliberately introduces tension as well as uncertainty about a win strategy. The game requires thirty to forty minutes; the de-briefing session (about the same time length) is essential.

Players

The game may be played by a group of four, eight, twelve, sixteen, or twenty players in four teams. (Four players would play individually, eight would play in pairs, twelve in teams of three, etc.) Any number of groups may play simultaneously but it is important that teams be seated or located far enough away from each other so that they can discuss their win strategy without being overheard.

A banker and a game director are needed. It is possible to combine the roles in one group, particularly if you are using single players rather than teams, but a separate banker will be needed for each group playing.

Materials

● 120 draughtsmen or poker chips (if using poker chips, you will need four of one colour and four of another, for indicating choices).

● a large copy of the pay-off formula, placed where it can be seen clearly by all players OR individual copies on 3" x 5" (8cm x 13cm) systems cards

● a stop watch or watch with a second hand

● paper and pencil for banker to record loans

● small table, if desired

Playing the game

1. The game director forms the group into four teams and seats or otherwise locates them in a square at least 6' across. Slightly more distance will be needed for teams than for single players.

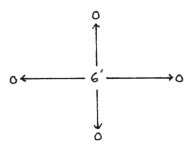

2. Display or distribute the pay-off formula and give the players about three minutes to study it. While they are becoming familiar with it, the banker distributes twelve draughtsmen or poker chips to each team. Two of the chips are the colours for indicating choices.

3. At the end of the three minutes, teams may discuss among themselves their understanding of the game for a further minute. They should then choose one person to present their choice during each round. If only four people are playing, omit discussions.

4. The game director reads aloud these directions:
a) "The title of this game is Pay-Off and your goal is to win as many chips (or draughtsmen) as you can.
b) You may not confer or communicate with any other player in any way unless given specific permission by the game director.

c) (To be read only if playing in teams). Teams must agree on a choice for each round. You will choose to play either red or black (substitute other colours if appropriate).

OR

(To be read only if playing individually). You will choose to play either red or black in each round (substitute other colours if appropriate).

d) You must retain at least one red and one black chip (substitute other colours if appropriate) for indicating choices. If you run out of chips, you may borrow from the bank.
e) You must keep your choice secret until you are asked to reveal it.
f) There are ten rounds in the game. During each round you will have one minute to confer with other members of your team to make your choice The time for round one begins now."

5. After the lapse of one minute, the game director asks each player or team to indicate the choice for that round. They may do so by holding the chip or draughtsman up where all can see, or by coming forward to place the chip onto a table in the middle of the square.

6. Pay-Off according to the formula.

7. Continue the game as above, allowing one minute for choosing in each round. (If playing individually, you may need only 20—30 seconds for this step.) Pay-off at the end of each round and allow time for borrowing from the bank.

8. At the beginning of round five, the game director should say: "Round five is a bonus round. All amounts won or lost in this round will be multiplied by three. Before you make your choice for this round, you may discuss the game with all the other players in the group. After the discussion you will have one minute to choose your colour for round five. The group conference begins now."

9. After three minutes, ask players to return to their original locations and resume playing as above. Remember to multiply the pay-off formula by three (for this round only).

10. Continue playing as above. Round eight is the same as round five, except that the pay-off is multiplied by five. Read the directions from Step 8 above, substituting five as the bonus value.

11. Round ten is the same as round five except that the pay-off is multiplied by ten. Read the directions from Step 8 above, substituting ten as the bonus value.

12. Players or teams count up their pay-off score (total chips in hand). Players must pay back all loans to the bank. If they are unable to repay the bank, their pay-off score is stated in minus terms.

13. Count up the net pay-off of the four players or teams. (For instance, +20+11−3−18=10, etc.)

De-briefing

An evaluation and de-briefing session is particularly important with this game since feelings may become heated over betrayal of trust.

1. What was the maximum group pay-off possible? (If all consistently chose black, the collaboration option, the group pay-off would be +100; that is, +25 for each of the four players or teams.)

2. Compare the actual group pay-off with the possible net of +100.

3. Did any players consider group pay-off, or did they think only of their own score?

4. Discuss the merits of collaboration versus competition. Read aloud again your instructions in 4a. above. Did everyone assume that the "you" meant you as a player or team, rather than you as a total group?

5. Did any player or team consistently betray the others? Were there any who stuck to agreements? Ask these players how they felt during the game. Talk about feelings until everyone has had a chance to express theirs.

6. Did any player or team attempt to cheat the bank? Did the banker chase up players for a losing pay-off, or did they initiate payment?

7. How does this model of behaviour relate to other situations? What can you learn from this game which will help you in your relationships with others? (Depending on your group and purpose, you might wish to be more specific. For instance, "What have we learned from this game which will help us in our family relationships?" Or, "How was this game situation like those we face in school?")

Other uses of Pay-Off

Pay-Off might be used to introduce a study on gambling, or in the midst of such a study, to provide a common experience. Play the game as directed, but only with single players (instead of teams). Use the bonus rounds, but do not have a consultation period before them. Discuss the game in terms of how it felt to win, or to lose. Talk about the development of a win strategy. Was there a strong drive to win? It would be fun to use play money for the pay-off.

In relationship with other games and exercises, Pay-Off may be used as a team-building exercise for a leadership team beginning a year's work, or for a group who want to become more closely knit, or in any instance when you wished to emphasize interdependency.

PAY-OFF FORMULA

4 reds	everyone loses 1 chip to bank
3 reds, 1 black	each red wins 1 chip from bank black loses 3 chips to bank
2 reds, 2 blacks	each red wins 2 chips from bank each black loses 2 chips to bank
1 red, 3 blacks	red wins 3 chips from bank each black loses 1 chip to bank
4 blacks	everyone wins 1 chip from bank

GETTING THERE!

A game for 3 to 8 players. Designed by Pat Baker.

GETTING THERE! is concerned with the means which people use in achieving their goals. The object of the game is to get from the start to THERE! The winner is the player who gets THERE! first.

Equipment

Playing board
Set of Choice or Chance cards
A counter for each player
One die or spinner

THE PLAYING BOARD
For the playing board you will need a sheet of paper or cardboard about 25 inches by 20 inches (63cm x 50cm). The board should be set out as in the diagram on page 41.

Gummed coloured paper discs about ¾" (1.5 cm) in diameter are ideal for marking the course, or you can draw directly on the playing board, using a ten- or twenty-cent coin as a template.

The main route from the start to THERE! is the one marked on the diagram with numbered circles and stars. The numbered circles should all be of one colour. (The playing instructions assume that pink has been chosen as the standard colour.) The un-numbered circles on the main route are hazards, and

should be a different colour, for example, red. Write on each of these the particular instruction given in the diagram (Go back 2 spaces, etc.). The stars should be of a different colour again.

The routes marked in the diagram with solid spots indicate the long way around. Use another colour, for example, blue. The routes marked with dotted circles are short cuts. Use a different colour again, for example, gold. Note that a couple of hazards are included in the short cuts. These should be the same colour as the hazards on the main route.

The area marked Choice or Chance should be big enough to take a pile of cards about 3" x 2" (8cm x 5cm).

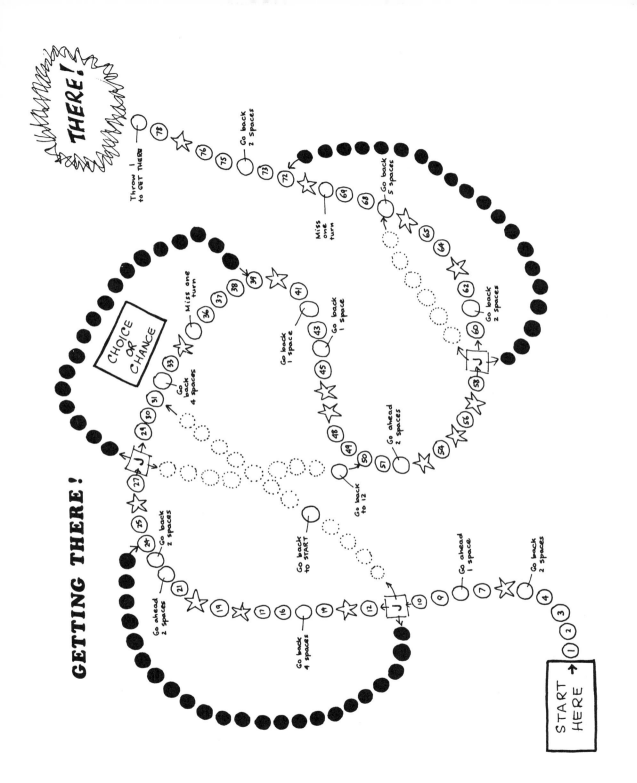

GETTING THERE!

THERE!

CHOICE OR CHANCE CARDS

Prepare a set of fifty cards, each about 3" x 2" (8cm x 5cm). Each one has an instruction written on it:

IT'S YOUR CHOICE. Either everyone moves forward 3 spaces, or you stay put and everyone else moves back 3 spaces.

HOLD THIS CARD until you are instructed to draw another one. At that time any penalties or advantages are doubled.

If your next throw is an even number, halve it. If it is an odd number, double it.

IT'S YOUR CHOICE. Either move the last player up to join you, or move the leader back to join you. If you move the last player up, you share his next advantage, whatever it may be. If you move the leader back, you share his next penalty.

No-one else may move forward until you reach space 39. If you have already passed there, you may not move forward until everyone else reaches space 39. HOLD THIS CARD until the action is completed.

Move to space 25. If this is a forward move, everyone else must go back 3 spaces. If it is a backward step, everyone else moves ahead 3 spaces.

Space 16 is your personal property as long as you HOLD THIS CARD. Any other player landing there must stay put on his next throw while you advance the number of spaces indicated by his throw. In addition, you may take refuge on space 16 at any time, rather than pay a penalty demanded by another player.

You and one other player chosen by you move forward 2 spaces each.

HOLD THIS CARD. When and if you land on space 29 all other players must retreat 2 spaces.

HOLD THIS CARD. Whenever any other player lands one space ahead of you, you may join him on that space. Should you choose not to do so, you must move back one space.

IT'S YOUR CHOICE. Everyone (including you) moves back one space, or you may move any one player back 5 spaces.

IT'S YOUR CHOICE. Either you take an extra turn or everyone else moves back instead of forward on their next throw.

No-one else may move on their next turn unless they throw a six. Each time a six is thrown, *you* move *back* six spaces. If no-one throws a six, you move six spaces forward as a bonus before your next throw.

IT'S YOUR CHOICE. Either advance to one space ahead of the player immediately ahead of you, or make him stay put until you catch up in the normal course of the game. HOLD THIS CARD until the action is completed.

IT'S YOUR CHOICE. Move forward 3 spaces or take an extra turn.

IT'S YOUR CHOICE. Either you may send everyone else back to at least 6 spaces behind you, or everyone but you must remain where they are until a 6 is thrown.

HOLD THIS CARD. When and if you land on space 38 you get an extra turn.

The space you are now on is your personal domain for as long as you HOLD THIS CARD. Any other player landing there must pay any penalty you decide to impose. In addition, you may choose to take refuge there at any time rather than pay a penalty demanded by another player.

HOLD THIS CARD. Give yourself room to manoeuvre. Whenever any-one lands on your space or on the space either side of you he is not allowed another throw until you are at least 5 spaces away.

IT'S YOUR CHOICE. Either you may move to space 41, or you may carry on as usual. If you choose space 41 you may not move forward again until you throw a 6.

IT'S YOUR CHOICE. Either send everyone else back 4 spaces, or HOLD THIS CARD to cancel out the next penalty you are given.

If any other player is within 10 spaces of GETTING THERE! he must move backwards on his next throw.

If any other player is holding a secret card, you may demand that it be revealed.

IT'S YOUR CHOICE. Either the leader and the last player swap places on the board, or you advance 2 spaces.

IT'S YOUR CHOICE. Either you take another turn, or everyone else moves back 2 spaces.

On their next throw, only those throwing odd numbers may move for-ward. Those throwing even numbers move backwards. This includes you!

HOLD THIS CARD. From now on, anyone who lands on the same space as you must pay a penalty. In each case, you may choose either to send him back 3 spaces or to make him miss one turn.

IT'S YOUR CHOICE. Either you move forward 5 spaces while everyone else stays put, or you may send one other player back 10 spaces while you stay put and everyone else moves forward 3 spaces.

IT'S YOUR CHOICE. Either you move back 2 spaces or miss a turn.

Bonus! Count double on your next throw.

Move to the nearest junction.

IT'S YOUR CHOICE. You may move up to join the leader, or you may send any one player back to join the tail-ender.

IT'S YOUR CHOICE. Either the leader moves back to one space behind the last player, or the last player moves up to one space ahead of the leader.

You may demand a card from any player who is holding one. If the player holds more than one, you may specify which one you want. Secret cards remain secret.

Blow! Drop back 3 spaces

Bonus!   Advance 4 spaces.

All cards being held by all other players must be returned to the pack without comment, and the pack shuffled. All advantages or penalties attached to the cards are cancelled.

IT'S YOUR CHOICE. Either move forward 4 spaces or take another card.

Disaster!   Drop back 10 spaces

Big deal!   Full ahead 1 space.

Secret. HOLD THIS CARD until you want to use it. When you present it to another player he must not move forward until he throws a 6.

Secret. HOLD THIS CARD. It has no significance, but it may make the others nervous!

Secret. Try a bluff. Tell the other players this card says whatever you like. If they believe you, good luck to you. If challenged, move back 5 spaces.

Secret. HOLD THIS CARD until you want to use it. It reverses any penalty imposed on you by another player, i.e. he pays the penalty and you receive any advantages associated with it!

IT'S YOUR CHOICE. Either you move forward 5 spaces, or everyone else moves back instead of forward on their next throw.

Secret. HOLD THIS CARD until you want to use it. Present it to a player who has thrown a 6 to make him move backwards instead of forward.

Secret. HOLD THIS CARD until you want to use it. When you choose to reveal it, everyone else must move backward on their next throw.

Secret. If you can persuade another player to trade positions with you on the board, all is well. Otherwise, back to space 1!

Secret. HOLD THIS CARD until you want to use it. When you choose to present it to another player, it sends him back to space 1. At the same time, you stay put, and everyone else advances 3 spaces.

Secret. One effective way of GETTING THERE! is to cheat a little. Try moving an extra space each time you advance your counter. If caught, apologize, miss one turn, and try honesty for a change!

Preparing to play

Lay out the playing board.

Shuffle the Choice or Chance cards and place the pack face down in the space marked on the board.

Choose counters and decide on order of play.

Rules

1. Each player in turn throws the die and advances the number of spaces indicated by his throw.

2. The regular route to THERE! is marked by the pink discs. The route includes a number of hazards (red discs) and choices/chances (silver stars).

3. When a player's throw lands him on a red disc, he must carry out the instructions written on it.

4. When a player's throw lands him on a star, he takes the top card from the Choice or Chance pack. Unless the card is marked SECRET, he reads it aloud and carries out the instructions. When the action is completed, the card is returned to the bottom of the pack. Should a SECRET card be drawn, it is not read aloud until the player chooses to make use of it, after which it is returned to the bottom of the pack.

5. JUNCTIONS are marked at three points on the playing board ("J"). Should a player land *on* a junction, he must choose whether to continue on the regular route or to take one of the two alternative routes (see 6 and 7 below). The choice does not apply when a player's throw takes him *through* a junction. In this case he must continue along the regular route.

6. A player landing on a junction may choose to take a short cut (marked with gold discs). However, while he is on this route, every other player draws a Choice or Chance card prior to making his own throw. This condition continues as long as any counter is on the short cut route. (Should more than one player be taking short cuts at the same time, other players draw the appropriate number of cards as their turns come round. For example, if two players are on short cuts, the rest of the players will draw 2 cards each, while those two players will be entitled to one card each.)

7. A player landing on a junction may choose to take the long way round (marked by blue discs). As long as his counter is on this route, he may not be penalized by any other player. At the same time, he may enjoy any advantages that are offered.

8. Should a situation arise which does not seem to be covered by the rules, players should negotiate to decide how it is to be resolved.

9. The game is over when the first player gets THERE! However, it may continue by mutual agreement until other players get THERE! too.

DON'T SKIP THIS – ITS IMPORTANT.

Reflect on the game experience.

Discuss these points:

How did you feel about playing the game? Did you care about the outcome?

On what basis did you make choices during the game?

How did you feel about the actions you took?

How did you feel about the other players and their actions?

Would you make the same kinds of choices in pursuing other goals?

Did you find it difficult to do mean things?

Were you pleased when someone else got slapped down?

Did you decide to continue the game after the first player got THERE! If so, why?

What did you learn about yourself from this game?

A simulation game for youth in a multi-racial society, reprinted from MOMENT, February 1972. Used by permission.

MANA is a human relations game.

It simulates certain features of society.
It dramatizes the place of youth in society.
It provides a way of learning about society.
It encourages reflection upon experience.

THE OBJECT of the game

is to reach MANA

the place where you have   power
                          status and
                          recognition.

Rules

1. MANA may be played by 4 to 10 players.

2. Each player starts with $200 and 3 Instruction Cards.

3. Each turn the player chooses one card, reads out the instructions, and moves accordingly.

4. After each move the player discards that card and picks up a new card from the card pile.

5. A player with a Criminal Record (having been in Jail or fined) must subtract one from every forward move and add one to every move backwards.

6. To get out of Drop Out or Commune you must pay $200.

7. To move into MANA you must have at least $500 debt free.

8. You may borrow money from other players.

9. The game does not end when someone reaches MANA but when you have finished a period of EVALUATION.

Equipment

Playing board
Set of Instruction Cards
Play money
A counter for each player

The design for the PLAYING BOARD is set out on page 48. Copy it onto a sheet of paper or cardboard about 20 inches by 15 inches (50cm x 48cm).

FOR PLAY MONEY you will need about $5000 in $100 units. Matches or tokens may be used to represent money.

Prepare a set of fifty INSTRUCTION CARDS, each about 3" x 2" (8cm x 5cm). Each card has an instruction written on it.

(Australian users will need to rewrite some of the instructions to suit their situation.)

You have been convicted and fined $400 for refusing to do Compulsory Military Training because you object to war. Pay $400 or go to Jail.

GO BACK TWO

You write off your father's car. Rather than face his wrath you go to a commune, and do not move for two rounds.

GO TO COMMUNE

The local paper does a series on the problems of youth. You are asked your opinions and you really lay it on thick about parents, the fuzz and oldies.

EVERYONE GO BACK TWO

Because of the local bylaws you are not allowed to start a Coffee Shop which will provide help for those in need of friendship and counselling.

GO BACK THREE

A famous guru convinces you that the reason that you are having trouble with the police and other authorities is due to the colour of your skin. You believe him and get very bitter about it.

GO BACK THREE

Your mother and father find that you are pregnant. They send you away to a distant relative and tell people that you have gone to work in the big city.

GO BACK THREE

You work hard, pass all your exams and get promoted to a high income. You get $100 now and next turn.

GO AHEAD FOUR

You are picked up at 3 a.m. for being "idle and disorderly" and are locked up. Your parents will not listen to your reasons and tell you what they think of you.

GO BACK FOUR

You manage to persuade your Elders that you run a teenage dance, if the police are informed and there is no liquor on the premises.

GO FORWARD TWO

This entitles you to get out of Jail. The authorities suddenly discover it has all been due to a terrible mistake.

GO OUT OF JAIL

Your Church protests against racial discrimination but does nothing to welcome members of another race to its meetings.

EVERYONE GO FORWARD ONE

You have so many criminal convictions that the Judge decides that you should not menace society any longer. You must stay in jail for four rounds.

GO TO JAIL

You disagree with your Elders in public. They humiliate you in return. You leave home and go flatting.

GO BACK THREE

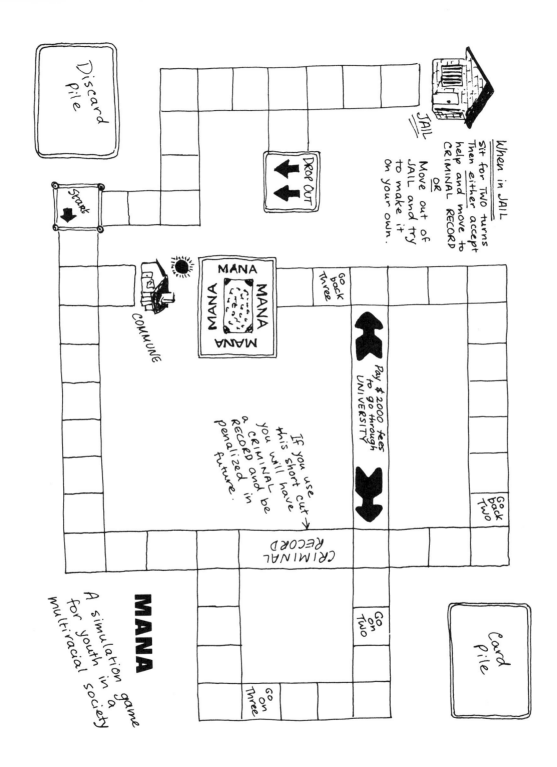

Discard Pile

JAIL

When in JAIL
Sit for TWO turns
Then either accept
help and move to
CRIMINAL RECORD
OR
Move out of
JAIL and try
to make it
on your own.

DROP OUT

Start

MANA MANA MANA MANA MANA

COMMUNE

Go back Three

Pay $2000 fees to go through UNIVERSITY

If you use this short cut you will have a CRIMINAL RECORD and be penalized in future.

CRIMINAL RECORD

Go back Two

Go on Two

Go on Three

MANA

A simulation game for youth in a multiracial society

Card Pile

You have a chance to take up an apprenticeship. If you take it you cannot move forward for three rounds when you receive $200. If you do not take it move —

FORWARD FOUR

You win a prize in the State Lottery. Collect $500

GO FORWARD THREE

You have been a good kid. Everybody likes you. You get a gift of $100. Do not move forward or get the money if you have been in trouble with the police.

GO AHEAD FOUR

You become a radical student. You only work long enough to get money to go to demos and to keep yourself dressed appropriately.

GO TO DROP OUT

You learn the Maori language at University but don't know any Maoris who can speak it.

GO FORWARD FOUR

You punch someone on the nose who says "Listen, I've nothing against Islanders, it's just that . . . " He charges you with assault. Pay $200 to one player who is doing well in the game.

GO BACK FOUR

You and your friends are picked up by the police on suspicion of being involved in a burglary. You are treated like criminals and feel resentful afterwards.

GO BACK FOUR

You sell all your possessions and give the money to poor players. You feel good but have no money.

GO AHEAD TWO

You sell your sordid story with appropriate exaggerations, to "The Truth". Receive $100.

GO AHEAD TWO

Your landlord complains for the last time about your noisy record player and parties. You are asked to leave.

GO BACK TWO

You keep your nose clean and your parents pay for you to go through University. Use this card at the appropriate time to get through University free. Or cash it in for $300 and

GO FORWARD THREE

A dynamic young MP gets elected in your area. He promises to do something for the youth of your area.

EVERYONE GO FORWARD TWO

You get drunk and are convicted of disturbing the peace. Pay $100 fine.

GO BACK ONE

You join the Jaycees or Young National Party and have a swinging time at parties and social occasions.

GO FORWARD FIVE

You bet $100 and win the double. Receive $1,000.

GO AHEAD SIX

The Jaycees pick you as the most promising young person of the year. You receive $300 and add three to your next three forward moves. (Not to be played by drop outs or those with a criminal record.)

GO AHEAD THREE

The dynamic young MP who was elected to represent your area finds that he is powerless to get his party to help the youth of your area.

EVERYBODY GO BACK TWO

You get a P.O. Bonus Bond issue of $100, for wisely investing your money. The bonus is tax free.

GO AHEAD THREE

Play this card next. You decide to drop out of society. Give your money to someone.

GO TO DROP OUT

You find it hard to get a job because of your looks and racial background. You complain to the authorities and are told that there is no such thing as racial discrimination in N.Z.

GO BACK THREE

You join a radical political group and dress and speak like them. Your friends and family regard you as a Communist.

GO BACK FOUR

You have a nine to five office job and study at night to improve your position. Suddenly you wonder what the point of it all is. You blow all your savings.

GO TO DROP OUT

Your boss has a sudden fit of generosity and gives you a bonus. You receive $100 unless you are a drop out, in jail, or at a commune.

GO AHEAD TWO

You take on a Hire Purchase agreement with an unscrupulous firm. You forget to pay one installment and they repossess. You lose everything you have paid and cannot afford a lawyer to fight it.

GO BACK FIVE

You have become an expert speaker on the subject of our multi-racial future. You are in demand by the media and spend a lot of time speaking to whites about the problem. Receive $200 journalist's fees.

GO AHEAD FIVE

You persuade the local Council to allow dancing in the streets and to decorate the town for a Mardi Gras.

GO FORWARD FIVE

Your community forms a Citizen's Advice Bureau. You offer to help with it.

EVERYONE GO FORWARD TWO

You join the Commune and find that you are accepted and valued as you are, without regard to race, hair, clothes or education.

GO TO COMMUNE AND GIVE MONEY AWAY

The flat you are staying in is raided by the police. One person is charged with possessing drugs. You are kept under surveillance.

GO BACK THREE

You organize a Woodstock for the Youth of your region. It is a good scene and provides a model of a style of life that all should be pursuing.

EVERYBODY GO AHEAD TWO

A TV documentary draws attention to your plight. Many people offer to help.

GO FORWARD THREE

You have recently come to NZ on a sponsored immigration scheme. You are bonded to work at a monotonous factory job for three years. You can't stand it and leave, causing all sorts of family and legal troubles.

GO BACK SIX

You lose all your money in a poker school. Pay over your money.

GO TO DROP OUT

Because you spend a lot of time with members of the local gang you have trouble getting a date for an important occasion.

GO BACK TWO

You join an antiwar demonstration. You get carried away (literally). You stay in jail overnight. In the morning you are released without being charged. You demand justice.

GO BACK FOUR

You risk all your money on the legal fees for defending a friend. He loses his case. Give all your money to the leading player.

GO BACK FIVE

You get a good job.
Receive $100

GO FORWARD THREE

Evaluation

At the conclusion of the game, reflect on the experience. Here are some questions to get you started:

What features of society does this game simulate?

How did you *feel* during the game?

How personally involved were you? Why was this?

What learning do you see in the game?

How will your behaviour be affected by the game?

How could this game be improved?

THE CONVICT GAME

Devised by Ian McCracken, and reprinted from LEARNING EXCHANGE No. 11. Used by permission.

About the game

There are many aids available to teachers who believe they can justify the teaching of the convict era, but few are primarily concerned with introducing students to the period. This game attempts to fill this gap by giving students the chance to build up some idea of the convict system without having to use more traditional teaching aids.

The game is mainly concerned with illustrating the various routes convicts took when they arrived in the eastern colonies and the hazards they encountered during sentence. For some students however, the experience has been wider. Some of the players have become emotionally involved in the game and have experienced jubilation or frustration depending on the hazards they encountered. Emotional experience of this nature has caused many students to make important judgments about individual convict punishments and the nature of the convict system in the Australian eastern colonies between 1788 and 1853.

The game has been constructed to operate on a simple hazard system. Each participant becomes a convict and follows one of the paths most convicts took during their period of punishment. Because the period remained fairly static between 1788 and 1853, it lends itself more readily to a game of this nature.

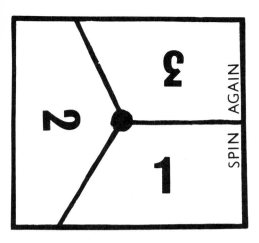

The game has a number of limitations none of which inhibit its effectiveness, but all of which players should be aware of.

Firstly, while it is correct to say that the system of convict punishment remained fairly static throughout the period, there were changes in the degree of application and the game does not illustrate this.

A second weakness concerns the regularity of punishment or favourable treatment. Both A.G.L. Shaw and L.L. Robson make figures available which illustrate the number of particular punishments carried out on groups of convicts, but no studies are available which follow the punishment inflicted upon individual convicts throughout their sentence. For students to gather adequate experience of the types of treatment within the three systems, more hazards or obstacles were placed in each of the three routes than was probably accurate for an ordinary term of punishment.

The third weakness relates to consistency. It is possible to encounter one or more hazards in Government Service, for example, which promote or encourage the convict/player for good behaviour; however, a few steps further on, the same convict/player may also be sent to a Penal Settlement for bad behaviour. Real life inconsistencies of this nature, I feel sure, would have been rare.

Rules

1. Form a circle of players around the board.

2. Each player select a piece to move with.

3. Taking turns in a clockwise order, spin the arrow. You will spin one, two or three.

4. In the first spin, each number constitutes a different route. Those who spin a *number one* have been sentenced to a place of Secondary Punishment and must follow the Penal Settlement route.

Those who spin *number two* have been assigned to a settler.

Those who spin *number three* must follow the Government Service route.

5. If a route has not been filled by a player at the beginning of the game, then the last player to enter the game must fill the vacant route. If two routes are left, then the last two players must fill the remaining two routes irrespective of the numbers they spin.

6. To finish the game, players must spin the exact number to gain a "ticket of leave".

7. As players encounter hazards the rest of the players must wait while the hazard is read out and its sentence carried out.

The playing board

The layout of the board is illustrated on page 54. It should be reproduced on a sheet at least 22" x 18" (55cm x 45cm). The route descriptions and hazards (see below) may be written directly onto the playing board or may be typed and stuck on.

Penal Settlements

Write the following description in the box labelled "Penal Settlements":

MOST CONVICTS HERE HAD BEEN TRANSPORTED A SECOND TIME OR WERE CONVICTED FOR SERIOUS CRIMES IN THE COLONIES. THE EMPHASIS WAS ON DISCIPLINE AND PUNISHMENT, NOT ON PRODUCTIVE LABOUR. PENAL SETTLEMENTS WERE SITUATED AT NORFOLK ISLAND, PORT JACKSON, EMU PLAINS, CASTLE HILL, TOONGABBIE, MACQUARIE HARBOUR AND PORT ARTHUR.

Each black square on the playing board constitutes a hazard. The following hazards should be marked on the Penal Settlement route:

3 Go back one space to receive fifty lashes for not doffing your cap to an Officer.

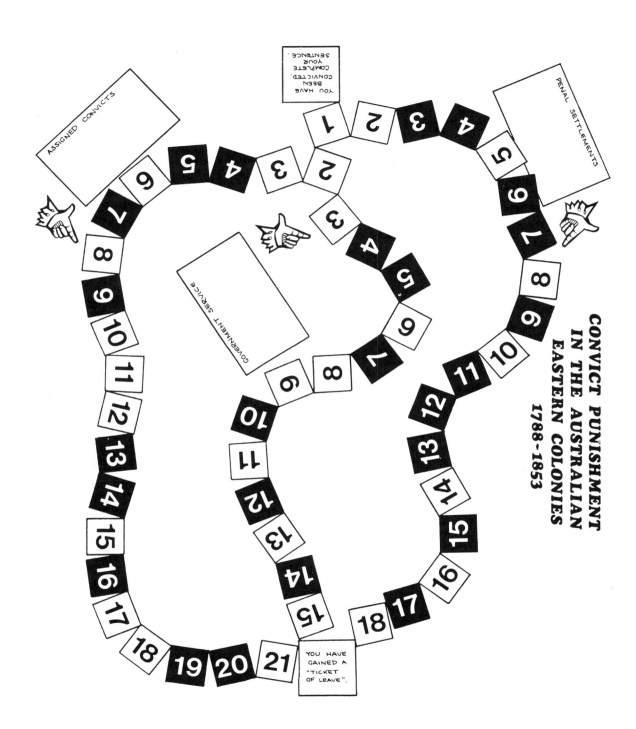

CONVICT PUNISHMENT
IN THE AUSTRALIAN
EASTERN COLONIES
1788-1853

ASSIGNED CONVICTS

PENAL SETTLEMENTS

GOVERNMENT SERVICE

YOU HAVE
BEEN
CONVICTED.
COMPLETE
YOUR
SENTENCE.

YOU HAVE
GAINED A
"TICKET
OF LEAVE".

4 Boils have developed on your ankles from the chains. Go back two spaces to receive medical treatment.

6 Answering an Officer back — miss one go to receive forty lashes and two days solitary confinement.

7 For attempting to escape you have just received five hundred lashes. Go back two spaces.

9 For your good behaviour you have been removed to number 6 Government Service.

11 Another prisoner has been found murdered; you are suspected. Go back three places to await trial.

12 Prison food is inadequate and you are suffering from malnutrition. Miss one go.

13 Because conditions here are so harsh, you have deliberately murdered a fellow prisoner to receive the death penalty. Leave the game.

15 You have been sentenced to hang for attempting to escape a third time. Leave the game; do not return.

17 You have not co-operated wth religious instruction and have refused to flog another prisoner. Go back three spaces to receive two hundred lashes.

Assigned Convicts

The following route description and hazards apply to the "Assigned Convicts" route:

THESE CONVICTS WERE DISTRIBUTED AMONGST THE SETTLERS. THEY WERE CLOTHED AND FED BY THEIR MASTERS AND WORKED THE SAME HOURS AS GOVERNMENT EMPLOYED CONVICTS. THIS GAVE THEM A FEW HOURS EACH DAY FOR EXTRA WORK OR FOR PLEASURE.

4 Your master has reported your misbehaviour and you have been punished by a magistrate. Go back one space.

5 Your master has ill-used you and you have been transferred to another farm. Go forward one space.

7 You have gained the knowledge of a trade. Go forward one space.

9 For taking part in criminal activities while under assignment you have been sent to number 10 in a Penal Settlement.

13 From working in your spare time you have saved extra money. Move on two places.

14 Your master is treating you well. Move on one place.

16 Your master overworks you. Go back one space.

19 You have left your assigned master after only three years and have now been sentenced to number 14 in a Penal Settlement.

20 Your building ability has been required in number 15 Government Service.

Government Service

The following route description and hazards apply to the "Government Service" route:

CONVICTS WERE SEPARATED INTO GANGS AND THEY WERE FED, CLOTHED AND LODGED BY THE GOVERNMENT. THEY WORKED ON GOVERNMENT PROJECTS INCLUDING ROADS, BRIDGES AND BUILDINGS. THEY BEGAN AT 6 A.M. AND WORKED UNTIL 3 P.M., THE REST OF THE TIME BEING THEIR OWN UNTIL THEY WERE LOCKED UP AT NIGHT.

4 You have been promoted from Gang Overseer to a Superintendent of three gangs. Go forward two places.

5 You have earned the job as a clerk or as a member of the police force for your continued good behaviour. Move forward one space.

7 For further misbehaviour you have been sentenced to the gaol gang and will now have to work a 12-hour day. Go back one space.

10 For your continued misbehaviour you have been sent to step 10 in a Penal Settlement.

12 You have misconducted yourself. Go back three spaces to receive two hundred lashes ordered by a magistrate.

14 From the work you have performed in your spare time (after 3 p.m. each day) you have saved a considerable amount of money. Move forward one space.

A game to help people in affluent countries understand some of the development problems of the Third World. Reprinted from DEED. Used by permission.

Poor man's cakewalk

Number of players: 2—10.

Materials needed

A playing board with 70 numbered spaces (see diagram). It should be large enough (e.g. 20″ x 25″ or 50cm x 57cm) for instructions to be written on the squares. For what is to be written, see below, under the heading "Playing Board".

A counter for each player.

One die.

To play

Players throw the die in turn and move forward the number of squares indicated by the throw. When a player lands on a square on which a situation is described, the description is read aloud and the player moves forward or back as instructed. If this move brings him to a square with further instructions, these also must be read and carried out. The game is finished when the first player reaches 70.

After the game, discuss:

What did the winner win?

How did you feel about the game?

Who or what were you competing against?

How did you feel about the other players?

What frustrations did you experience?

What have you learned about development problems?

Playing board

Write the following descriptions and instructions on the board:

Number
of Square

3 You die before your first birthday — like 20% of the children born in the developing world. For the purposes of the game, go back to square 1.

64	65	66	67	68	69	70
63	62	61	60	59	58	57
50	51	52	53	54	55	56
49	48	47	46	45	44	43
36	37	38	39	40	41	42
35	34	33	32	31	30	29
22	23	24	25	26	27	28
21	20	19	18	17	16	15
8	9	10	11	12	13	14
7	6	5	4	3	2	1

6 Favourable weather. You help your country to grow more coffee, sugar, bananas, cocoa, tea, sisal or jute. The warehouses are full. Move forward to 17.

10 You can't get enough of the right kind of food. You feel dull and drained of energy. You cannot work at your best. Go back to 4.

11 Your country achieves the United Nations target of a 6% annual economic growth rate and the president receives a telegram of congratulations from Kurt Waldheim. Advance to 28.

13 Green Revolution comes to your area. Can you afford seeds and fertilizers? Bumper crops — prices fall — rich gain — poor lose. Shake dice: if odd — forward; if even — back.

15 Your sons decide to leave the village and seek paid employment and a more exciting life in the city. You are left without help in the fields. Go back to 13.

17 World prices for agricultural commodities slump. Your country is 75% dependent on these commodities for its export earnings. Slide back to 5.

20 The benefits of your country's increasing wealth are not equally distributed. The already rich and educated in your country gain. You and your family miss out. Go back to 12.

22 Your country receives aid from a small Scandinavian country. It fills a gap in your nation's 5-year development programme. Go forward to 26.

23 Your country receives aid from a rich European nation. A cabinet minister flies off to negotiate the details. You move forward to 38.

24 Part of the aid your country receives from a nearby rich nation involves sending young people there for specialist training. Many of them are staying in the host country after their training is completed. Go back to 18.

26 The aid your country has received is an outright grant. There are no repayments to make. Advance to 37.

28 Population increases mean that your nation's increasing wealth has to be more thinly spread. Health and education services are hopelessly over-stretched. Go back to 20.

30 Aid has helped to import machines, created few jobs, and drawn more people into the cities. Have you gained? Shake dice: if even — forward; if odd — back.

32 Your government nationalizes foreign interests. Aid is frozen. Economic retaliation follows. Shake dice: if even — move forward; if odd — back.

34 Your country begins paying back interest and capital on loans under rich countries' aid programmes. Go back to 30.

36 Your country's plans to bring in land reform and grant credit facilities to small farmers is effectively blocked by vested interests at regional government level. Go back to 22.

38 The aid your country has received is tied to the purchase of the donor country's exports — which may not be the cheapest or the best for your purpose. Go back to 34.

40 Your government makes a stand on principle over a major foreign policy issue. A rich country retaliates by withdrawing all its aid. Shake dice: if even — forward; if odd — back.

41 Your country decides to invest in manufacturing industries to provide more export revenue, and less dependence on raw materials. Move on to 49.

43 Certain rich countries decide to allow your manufactured exports in duty free. But there is a long list of important exceptions. Move forward one square.

45 Tanks appear in the streets. A loudspeaker tells you to stay indoors. A new president speaks on the radio. Shake dice again: if odd — move forward; if even — back.

47 Your new export drive runs into a wall of tariff barriers and quotas when you try to sell to rich countries. Go back to 43.

48 Domestic political difficulties cause the legislature of a wealthy nation to trim its foreign aid programme. Will you be affected? Throw dice: if odd — move forward; if even — go back.

49 Your country's attempt to start manufacturing industries runs into trouble. You are short of capital, skilled labour and technical know how. Go back 2 squares.

51 Expensive new machines put you out of a job. There is no unemployment pay and there are no social services to fall back on. Go back to 23.

53 You have passed your exams and won a place at university. Go to square 57.

55 There is a freak storm. Floods ruin half the crop. There is no insurance money. Go back to 22.

57 You become a graduate. But there are no jobs for graduates. Go back to 52.

59 Inflation in the west pushes up the price of your country's essential imports. There is no corresponding rise in the price you are paid for your exports. So go back to 23.

61 You read in a paper that a firm in Europe has developed a new synthetic substitute for one of your country's main products. Go back 2 squares.

63 Your country begins to spend more and more on sophisticated armaments and expensive prestige projects. Essential social services are again set back. Return to 41.

64 Your country forms a common market with other developing nations. You increase trade between yourselves and your bargaining with the rich nations. Forward 4 squares.

65 Your country has become overloaded with foreign debts. You are paying back more money to the rich than you receive in aid. Go back to 23.

67 Development has led to extremes of social inequality. Social unrest leads to rioting in the streets and brings your country to the brink of civil war. Go back to 41.

69 Your government decides on a policy of stressing agricultural development and putting priority on appropriate labour intensive technologies. Go forward one square.

70 The United Nations now classifies your country as "developed". But there are still many poor people and a whole set of new problems is beginning.

This game is also available in package form from ACTION FOR WORLD DEVELOPMENT, P.O. Box 124, Brickfield Hill, N.S.W., 2000.

monopoly

Topic: Attitudes toward poverty.

Purpose: To concretize economic discrimination against minorities.

Have enough Monopoly games so that the entire group can play the game. Before beginning each group should draw up a new set of rules, in which half the players belong to a dark-skinned minority group and half are whites. The rules should favour the whites and impair the others' chance of winning. This experiment might be used in conjunction with a study of the existing conditions in the city or might introduce such a research project.

In devising the game, students can compose different sets of Chance and Community Chest cards, establish different fees that the players receive when passing Go, decide on different criteria for going to and getting out of jail, and zone certain neighbourhoods "For Whites Only". Rules should be based on existing conditions insofar as possible. Students should be given the opportunity to play the game from both sides, and feelings should be discussed when the game is finished.

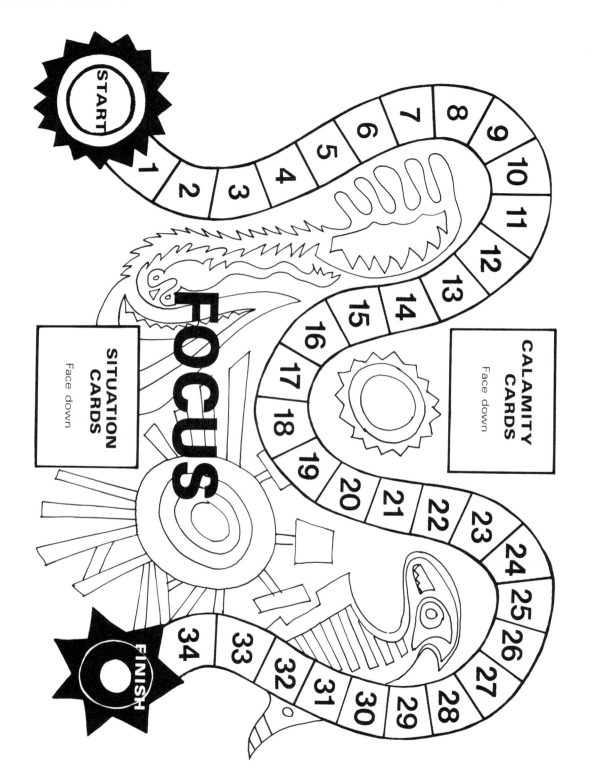

START

1 2 3 4 5 6 7 8 9 10 11 12 13 14 15 16 17 18 19 20 21 22 23 24 25 26 27 28 29 30 31 32 33 34

FINISH

FOCUS

SITUATION CARDS
Face down

CALAMITY CARDS
Face down

FOCUS

A game developed by Nancy Anderson for the Focus '73 conference. Reprinted by permission of Methodist Overseas Missions, Melbourne.

Aim

Focus is a game which aims to help people become involved in some of the tensions and problems being faced by indigenous leaders in a country such as Papua New Guinea.

Role

In this game you are asked to play the part of Demas and try to make the decisions you think he would make.

Demas

Demas is a market gardener. He also owns two trucks which he uses for carrying produce to market and for hiring to other people. He lives only a few miles from the town. He is a member of the Local Government Council and is on the Finance Committee of the Local Church. Demas' wife Moli has had leprosy and attends the hospital for regular treatment. She and their two eldest children help Demas in their business. The other two children attend primary school.

Rules

1. Up to six people can play the game (or more than six can play in teams). If teams are used, members must reach a group decision before voting, and a representative of the team will cast the team's vote.

2. Each player has a counter (or jelly baby) to move on the board.

3. Players take turns to throw the die and move their counters.

4. If a player lands on a shaded square, play ceases while he takes the top Situation Card and reads it aloud. He then announces his choice from the alternatives given, remembering that he must try to think of the situation from the point of view of Demas. (The choice must be made from the alternatives offered. Players may not change or add to them.) If other players agree that he has chosen the best course of action for Demas they will raise their hands. If they disagree they will fold their arms.

5. A player moves forward two squares if everyone has raised his hand. He moves back two squares if everyone has folded his arms. However, if voting is mixed he moves forward one square.

6. When a player throws a one, play ceases while that player takes up a Calamity Card and reads it aloud. *Each* player gives a brief statement of how he would act in that situation. Players vote to choose the best answer and that player moves on three spaces. No one else moves. The player who threw the one does *not* move forward one space. If the player who has moved forward lands on a shaded square he takes a situation card and play proceeds in the usual way.

7. Play continues until (a) the time is up OR (b) one of the players finishes the course.

Reflection

Allow at least fifteen to twenty minutes at the end of the game so that players can share with each other as they reflect on the game. Questions like these may help:

What have you learned from playing this game?

What situations did you find most difficult? Why?

Did you try to respond as you thought Demas would? Or as you would yourself? Were you aware of any difference between your own response and the one you thought Demas would give?

How can we become more sensitive to the problems and tensions of leaders in a country like Papua New Guinea? And what are we supposed to do about them anyway?

SITUATION CARDS

A The teachers of the Primary School have offered to run night classes for adults to learn simple English and Mathematics. The people in your area do not want to attend as they see no need for more education. You —

(a) tell the teachers to forget about night classes.

(b) enrol for classes yourself and hope others will follow your example.

(c) ask one of the teachers to explain to the people the value of the classes.

(d) use your influence to force selected people to attend.

B Your wife has been chosen to go to a conference for women from several Pacific countries. Medically it will not harm her (or others). She is shy and feels it would be better for someone else to go. You —

(a) force her to go.

(b) tell her not to go.

(c) discuss with her the reasons why she doesn't want to go and help her to overcome these.

(d) tell her to make up her own mind.

C You have recently attended the annual church assembly and were amazed to hear many younger men criticising the work done by the white missionaries in former years. You told these young men —

(a) "It is wrong to blame the white men; you should feel very grateful for all they have done."

(b) "Yes, maybe they made some mistakes but we are better off now than we used to be."

(c) "When you learn that you don't have to be grateful, then you are beginning to grow up."

(d) "It is always easy to look back and see how things should have been!"

D In the market you continually notice the rude manner in which many white people approach those who sell vegetables to them. This makes you very sad and angry. You decide you will —

(a) bring the matter to the notice of the council.

(b) tell the people to refuse to sell their goods to these rude people.

(c) shout angrily every time you see this kind of behaviour.

(d) not do anything about the situation.

E According to the old customs you are responsible for your sister's children. According to the new customs you feel a growing responsibility to provide for your own children. Two of your sister's seven children are now at High School and one will be getting married soon. You decide —

(a) that you must suffer the embarrassment of explaining to your sister that your finances are limited.

(b) to ask your wife's relations to give more support for your children.

(c) to place a limit on what you will give for each child.

(d) to follow either the old or the new customs, not both.

F You have been asked to serve on a Committee which is looking into the Primary School Curriculum and making suggestions for alterations. The change you would most like to see is —

(a) more agricultural training.

(b) less English and more use of your own language.

(c) more emphasis on current events.

(d) more religious training.

G According to the old customs you are responsible for helping to see that your sister's daughter marries a suitable young man. Nowadays many young people are making this decision for themselves. What will you do?

(a) tell the girl to choose whoever she likes.

(b) do nothing and see what happens.

(c) demand that she accept the man you have already chosen.

(d) try to find out which young men she is interested in and determine if any of them are suitable. Then advise her accordingly.

H Because of your position in the community you are expected to attend many official occasions. You feel you should dress well but are concerned because you don't want your people to feel you are showing off or seeking status. You therefore decide to —

(a) wear old clothes when you visit village people.

(b) show by your manner that you can dress well but still be friendly.

(c) wear ordinary clothes to the official occasions.

(d) stay home more often.

I A government welfare worker is at present conducting a survey of the problems of the young people who have finished Primary School but have not gone on to High School. You tell him that the best solution to the problem is to —

(a) set up community schools run by the people in the village.

(b) start National Service Projects on road and bridge building.

(c) have more night schools so they can study for higher exams.

(d) provide grants for youth clubs.

J An anthropologist spent three days in your village recently. His visit coincided with the time when many people were suffering from the effects of smallpox vaccinations. He wrote an article for the newspaper mentioning the "slow-thinking, slow-moving" people of your village. You —

(a) are glad that very few people in your village can read the newspaper!

(b) refuse to encourage any more overseas visitors to come to your village.

(c) write a letter to the newspaper condemning him and giving the full story.

(d) ignore the whole thing.

K A recent health survey shows that only 28% of the people in your area are eating sufficient protein. There are several things you could do to improve the situation. You decide —

(a) to allow school children to plant peanuts on your land.

(b) to ask infant welfare sisters to give talks about nutrition at the Women's Club meetings.

(c) to buy some fowls and encourage young people to breed poultry.

(d) to buy cases of tinned meat and fish and sell it as cheaply as possible.

L Some of the young people have been away to a youth camp where they saw guitars being used in worship services. When they suggested that this be tried at the local church it was opposed. You decide that the best way to help this situation is to —

(a) buy five guitars and donate them to the church.

(b) suggest that a camp for the older people be organised and that people from your village attend.

(c) hold a meeting to discuss the issue.

(d) arrange other opportunities for the young people to use their guitars.

M One of your Australian friends wants to bring his parents to see your village. You have invited them to your home for a meal. Your wife says she will not eat with you and the visitors, but you are keen for her to do so. How will you win her to your point of view?

(a) tell her you are the boss!

(b) explain what happens when you eat with your Australian friends.

(c) tell her you are proud of her and want the visitors to get to know her too.

(d) tell her they will be very uncomfortable if she doesn't sit with you all.

N Your youngest child has won a scholarship to a special school for bright children. This means she will have to travel to town and wear shoes every day, but will have the advantage of learning in a multi-racial class. What is your greatest fear?

(a) that she will grow away from her own culture?

(b) that she will marry someone from a different culture?

(c) that she will become proud of her achievements and grow past the rest of the family?

(d) that she will not cope?

O The elections are only three months away. Voting is not compulsory. You decide that you will —

(a) not vote.

(b) stand for election.

(c) join a political party.

(d) campaign for the party of your choice.

P The new volunteer from Australia wears brief bikinis in public places. This is causing a lot of talk among the people. The women are embarrassed and the men irate. You decide you will —

(a) explain carefully to her the customs of the people and the reaction to her clothing.

(b) tell the people not to stare.

(c) complain to the church official who is responsible for her.

(d) not do anything as it is not your business.

Q You have an opportunity for further training. This means you would have to be separated from your family for 8 months. You decide that you will —

(a) reject the offer.

(b) accept but make enquiries about accommodation for the family.

(c) accept the offer.

(d) accept on the condition that accommodation be found for your family.

R The local people are very upset and come to you for advice. A tourist ship is due in to the nearest port and the tourist officers have asked that the people perform as entertainment an ancient ritual which was an important part of their traditional religion. They will receive a percentage of the profits, and may sell artifacts to the tourists. You advise the people —

(a) to perform it but to explain its significance to the tourists.

(b) not to perform the ritual.

(c) to obey the officials and perform the ritual.

(d) to perform it, but to protest through the Council later.

CALAMITY CARD 1

In a nearby village the people are talking about a great bird who will fly down bringing cargo to them on a certain day. They have stopped work in their gardens and are waiting for its arrival. Many of your friends are talking about joining them.

What will you do in this situation?

CALAMITY CARD 2

Children playing with fire in a kitchen cause a huge blaze which sweeps quickly through the village. No-one is seriously hurt but many people have lost all their possessions.

Government officials arrive to list damages incurred by individuals. You overhear many people claiming to have lost much more than they really did.

What will you do?

CALAMITY CARD 3

A severe earthquake has shaken your area, destroying some buildings and upsetting the people. You try to carry on your work as well as you can but some of the people are very superstitious and refuse to co-operate with you. A rumour has spread around that the end of the world is coming in a couple of days.

What will you do?

CALAMITY CARD 4

In the market last Saturday a man from another part of the country made suggestive gestures to a couple of young women. The women's relatives became very upset and chased the strangers out of the market causing a great commotion. The police intervened but no action was taken. You have heard since that people are sharpening knives and spears.

What will you do?

CALAMITY CARD 5

Representatives of a large mining company have been surveying the land in your area. Some of the people are watching anxiously. They do not want to lose their land. Trouble starts when officials from the government and the mining company arrive to talk with the village elders about purchasing the land. Some of the younger men refuse to allow them to come near the village; they throw stones at the cars and shout angrily.

What can you do in this situation?

CALAMITY CARD 6

Entering the village one evening you notice that quite a large group of people is gathered around a radio. You learn that they have just heard that a visiting Australian has stated that Independence is only a few months away. Someone asks you if that means that all the white people will have to leave the country.

What will you tell them?
What does independence mean?

CALAMITY CARD 7

A plane crashed last night on the mountain behind your village. You want to lead a group of men to try to find it and help any survivors. But the local people have always been frightened of going on this mountain.

What can you do?

CALAMITY CARD 8

There is a 'flu epidemic in the area. Several babies and old people have died; many are very sick. You are keen to help but realize that there are others more qualified to do so.

What can you do to help?

CALAMITY CARD 9

Just recently quite a bit of property has been destroyed by vandals. You have been very outspoken in meetings about the need for them to be caught and punished. One night you catch your nephew coming out of the school window with torn up books.

What action do you take?

CALAMITY CARD 10

The people in your area belong to either the Catholic or the Protestant Church. Now there seems to be a number of new ideas being spread around by people belonging to the Bahai, Jehovah's Witness, Mormon, Seventh Day Adventist and Pentecostal sects.

People are confused and ask your advice as to the true Church.

What do you reply?

CALAMITY CARD 11

Your village is situated at one of the most beautiful beaches along the coast. It attracts many tourists who litter the beach with beer cans and bring their speed boats in where the little children usually play. The men of your village erected a fence across the road to prevent cars coming through your village. A car carrying three Australians and two Chinese men breaks down the fence. The people are getting very angry.

What will you do?

CALAMITY CARD 12

You have heard that only one-third of children who finish Primary School this year will be able to go on to Secondary School next year. You and members of the Local Government Council are upset about this.

What can you do?

CHRISTLIFESTYLE

The basic idea for this game comes from *Thumbs Up!,* a training game for camp leaders.

The purpose of the game is to help the participants think through situations in which their Christian commitment and lifestyle may be challenged and to make appropriate responses.

You will need to make a playing board and a set of situation cards. Set out the board as in the diagram. For the situation cards you will need cards about 3'' x 2'' (8cm x 5cm), in three different colours to correspond with the colours on the playing board. Make about fifteen to twenty cards of each colour.

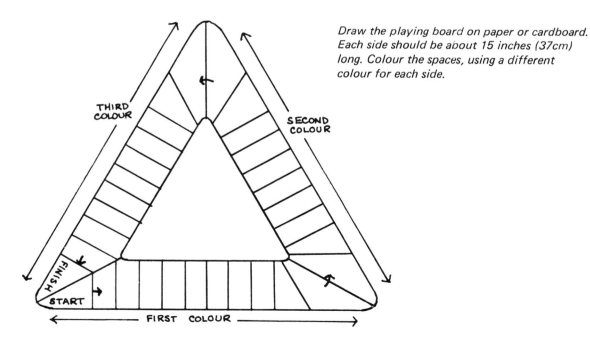

Draw the playing board on paper or cardboard. Each side should be about 15 inches (37cm) long. Colour the spaces, using a different colour for each side.

THIRD COLOUR

SECOND COLOUR

FINISH

START

FIRST COLOUR

The preparation of the situation cards is a task for the whole group. Each card should have written on it a description of a situation in which a young Christian may feel that he has to make a stand *as a Christian.* Here are some examples:

- You go to a party with a friend. You notice that a cigarette is being handed around. You detect a funny smell just as it comes to your hand. You realise it is marijuana.

- It is your first week in a new job. The young man at the next desk makes a habit of using language which you regard as blasphemous.

- The sports' club picnic is planned for Sunday morning when you would normally be in church.

- "The church is full of hypocrites", one of your friends says.

- "Sure Jesus was a great teacher", says a friend, "but I can't believe he was any more than that."

- "I don't see how anyone today could possibly believe in God", says a friend.

It will simplify the next step if each situation is written on a separate piece of paper. You will probably get the best output if you work in pairs or threes and pool the results.

Discard any duplications. Then go through the situation sheets, putting them into three piles according to the difficulty of the situations described. When you have done that, juggle the papers around a bit until the piles are about even. Then take the pile with the least difficult situations. Copy each of these onto a separate card, using cards of the same colour as the first section of the playing board. The second group of situations go on cards of the second colour, and the toughest situations on the third colour.

Now you are ready to play. Up to about ten people can take part.

Shuffle each group of cards and place them face down in the middle of the playing board. Each person places a counter on START. The first player takes the top card from the first pile and reads it aloud. He has one minute to think about his response, and then another minute to say what he would do or say in that situation. At a signal from the leader, all other players vote either thumbs up or thumbs down on his response. The difference between the number of thumbs up and thumbs down is noted, and the player moves forward or backwards that number of spaces. This happens to each player in turn. That is, he takes the top card from the first pile, thinks, responds, received a thumbs up or thumbs down signal from the rest of the players, and moves his counter accordingly. When each player has had a turn, the first player takes another card, and so on. Used cards are returned to the bottom of the pile.

A player always draws from the pile matching the colour of the space occupied by his counter. That is, on the first section of the course he draws from the first pile and deals with comparatively simple situations. As he progresses around the course he meets with tougher problems.

Although a playing course is used, the competitive element should not be stressed. The game is not to be regarded as a race between the players. If a player competes at all, it is with himself.

CAMP LEADERS' TRAINING GAME

An Australian group has designed a set of cards for a training game similar to THUMBS UP! (described briefly on page 94).

The purpose of the game is to help prospective camp leaders think through situations which may arise during a camp and decide how they would respond in such cases.

Playing board: as on page 66.

Cards: The following information should be transferred to cards approximately 5cm x 8cm. The cards should be of three different colours, corresponding with the three colours on the playing board.

The play: Follow the procedure set down on page 67 for playing "Christlifestyle".

One of your twelve-year-old campers arrives with about $5 worth of sweets which he shares with the others. In the middle of the week, another parcel of sweets arrives in the mail for this same camper. The other campers, and the sweets owner, are not eating very good meals, and two campers have had stomach aches. What do you do?

SET 1 (first colour):

The camp of which you are now director has a long-standing tradition of ghost stories around the campfire. Some of the leaders have some really scary ones. After one night of stories, seven campers have nightmares or wake up screaming. What do you do?

You are director of a mixed sex camp. Some of the girl campers have told you that some of the boys were looking in their windows late at night. What do you say to the girls? What — if anything — do you do?

You are a camp leader. One of the campers is so homesick that it is affecting the other campers. How do you deal with the homesickness?

One of the leaders in your camp does not pull his weight, but wanders off, not accepting his responsibility with the campers. He leaves most things to his co-leader. As camp director, what do you say to him?

It is quite cold at camp, and some kids absolutely refuse to have a shower or a swim to clean themselves wholly. By the third day some of them have begun to smell quite strongly. As camp director, how do you deal with the situation?

You are the leader of a small group of ten-year-olds and you realize that the kids are not having regular bowel movements. This is causing a general lassitude, back aches, etc. You suspect it is because they are not used to using latrines. What do you do?

In your camp there are junior leaders (leaders-in-training) who are breaking some fairly important camp rules. This has come to the notice of the younger campers, and some of them have mentioned it to you, as camp director. What do you say to the campers who report it to you? What do you say to the junior leaders?

You are the camp director and one of the leaders tells you that he is worried about a ten-year-old camper who displays what he calls "homo-sexual tendencies". This is mainly seen in his desire to kiss all the other boys goodnight. What do you say to the leader? What — if anything — do you say to the camper? to the other campers in the group?

Quite by accident, you discover that one of the campers in your small group is stealing from other group members. In the general confusion of the cabin, no one has noticed anything missing yet, but one or two have said they can't find something. What do you do?

As director of an unstructured camp, you find that some of the campers in the small groups are not staying with their own group, or following the programme which they, as a group, suggested to the group leaders. How do you deal with this problem?

You are the director of a youth camp. One of your leaders is in charge of a group in which his girlfriend is present. It is obvious to everyone that he is ignoring the rest of the group and spending his time with her. What do you do about it?

SET 2 (second colour):

You are camp director. A camper has reported to you that some of the male camp leaders have brought some beer into the camp for the female leaders. What do you say to the camper who reports it to you? What do you say to the leaders?

One leader objects strongly to the methods being used at the camp and he seems to be leading his group away from the objectives of the camp. As camp director, how do you deal with this?

You are camp director, in charge of a number of fairly young leaders. You find that it is very difficult to develop a differentiation between leader and group. How can you help the leaders in their role?

One camper will not mix in with the others but will only call them names. He wanders off with simple excuses when work needs to be done. He seems to be in a dream a lot of the time. As his group leader, how would you deal with the problem?

On the third day of a week-long camp, you are all completely drenched. It has rained day and night and you have a shortage of sheltered space and equipment. Should you abandon the camp?

A letter from the parents of one of your campers has stressed the import-ance of his taking allergy tablets with each meal. You find it is very difficult to get him to take the tablets, and suspect that he is lying about having taken them. How do you deal with this?

One of the male leaders has become personally involved with a girl camper and it is affecting his approach to his leadership role. You are the camp director. What do you say to the leader?

You, as a group leader, are landed with a bunch of campers who only came to camp to get away from home. They say "No" to every programme idea you suggest. How do you deal with them?

One of your campers is a child from an undisciplined family, where the general rule has been permissiveness. Naturally the camper acts the same way in the group. As his leader, how do you deal with his unruly behaviour?

You are a camp director with all male leaders (and all male campers) and two female cooks. You find that some of the male leaders are beginning to spend a lot of time in the kitchen with the cooks, and with them in other instances, so much so that the leaders are neglecting their duties. What do you do?

You have a camp with a set theme of Swagman's Camp. It rains every day. How do you keep the theme of this camp alive?

You are a camp director. One of your leaders tends to sarcasm when dealing with behaviour problems. As camp director, how do you deal with (a) the leader, and (b) a camper who is upset by the leader's sarcasm?

SET 3 (third colour):

A visitor comes to the camp, bringing alcohol which is banned on the campsite. He shares it with some of the leaders. As camp director, what do you say to (a) the visitor, and (b) the leaders?

You are the director of a mixed sex camp of 10—12-year-olds, who have the whole of the evening programme together. Boys and girls have been disappearing together, and you are hearing stories about the sexual experiments these kids have been trying. How do you deal with this?

A leader is over-anxious about giving the boys in his group sex education. As a result, he is labelled as "homosexual". As camp director, what do you do?

You are director of a camp, and you find out that some of your leaders are undermining your authority behind your back. What do you do?

The leaders in your camp are trying to outdo each other in the accomplishments of their groups. As a result, the campers are becoming merely instruments of the leaders. What can you, the director, do about it?

As director of a mixed sex camp, you find yourself very attracted to one of the leaders of the opposite sex. This is the only chance you'll have to get to know each other. What do you do?

On the second night of a week-long camp of fifty 11—13-year-olds, two brothers both come down with chicken pox. A little investigation shows that 12 more of the campers are in the school class of one or the other of the boys. What do you do?

You are a camp director, and have various leaders leading different skill groups. Some leaders think that other leaders are incompetent, and try to cover territory they think the campers are missing out on. This has given the campers the idea that various leaders are no good. How do you deal with this situation?

One of the campers is a loner with family background problems. What can be done to include the camper with the group when all efforts so far to get him/her to join in have been adamantly rejected by the camper? As group leader, what do you do?

A short-term visitor joins one of the groups and leads the campers in that group in making trouble. As the group's leader, how do you deal with the problem?

You have a camper who, though not retarded, is slow mentally, and is being teased, tormented, and physically hurt by the other campers. Do you isolate him in some way from the main group? Or how else do you deal with the problem?

You are the director of a camp, and have planned a programme with which your associate director is distinctly unhappy, although the rest of the leaders are quite happy. You find that your associate is criticizing the programme behind your back and generally spreading ill will. What do you do?

SURVIVAL SHELTER

This game is an adaptation of an adaptation of an adaption of a NASA exercise! Pat Baker is responsible for this version.

The goal of the game is to give the players an experience of co-operative decision-making, and an opportunity to consider and express values.

Any number can play. The only materials needed are a pencil/pen and paper for each player. Divide into groups of three to four and set the scene:

World War III has begun. A nuclear attack on this area is imminent. The people in your group will be sharing a survival shelter for an indefinite period. The shelter is equipped with basic requirements for physical survival and health.

Even though conditions will be somewhat cramped, it is anticipated that each member of the group will be able to bring to the shelter an unspecified number of items which he/she believes will be of value in the situation. Each person should now list up to 10 items which he/she would like to bring. Take about 5 minutes for the listing.

* * * * * *

It is unlikely that there will be (a) enough room in the shelter, (b) time, for each person to bring all the items he/she has listed. Therefore it is necessary to establish priorities. Take 3–5 minutes to go over your lists and number the items in order of priority. Do this individually.

* * * * * *

Latest reports suggest that you will have to take refuge in the survival shelter within the next twenty-four hours. Meet with the other members of the group to decide which items from the individual lists may be brought. (You will not know until the last minute exactly how many extra items can be accommodated in the shelter. Work on the assumption that it will be between five and ten items. For the purposes of the exercise, size and weight do not matter.) Take 10–15 minutes to draw up a list, in

priority order, of up to ten items, taking into account each item's value to an individual and value to the group. Voting is *not* permitted: try to reach agreement in some other way.

After the game think about these things:

On what basis were the decisions made?

How seriously did you take the individual priority lists?

Were the items finally chosen more for their importance to particular members of the group, or because they might benefit the group as a whole?

How difficult was it to make the choice?

Did each person have an opportunity to plead for the items on his/her own list?

Did people listen to what others had to say?

Were everyone's needs considered?

Did any one person make the decisions, or was there general agreement?

Did anyone feel that the final decision was unfair?

How did people feel about the way the decisions were made?

How could the decision-making process have been improved?

How do you think the group would function together if you really were thrust into a survival situation?

$PREE !

A game for any number of participants, devised by Pat Baker.

What would you do if you suddenly came into money? Would you spend it? save it? invest it? give it away? This is what SPREE! is all about. Each participant receives a "legacy" and is immediately confronted with a mass of options in the shape of letters, memos, advertisements, appeals, etc. During the next 30—45 minutes he must make a decision about each item.

Although SPREE! is concerned with the use of imaginary money, it relates very closely to our real attitudes, priorities, and values. The sharing session at the end of the exercise will allow participants to say what they feel about the money and possessions they actually have as well as those they can only imagine.

Preparation

SPREE SHEETS

Each participant will need one SPREE SHEET. This should be at least quarto size. At the top of the sheet, the amount and terms of the legacy are already written when the participant receives it. The rest of the sheet is blank. During the game, the participant will use it to note his decisions.

Not all legacies need be the same. In fact, it will add interest to the sharing session if there has been diversity at this point. The following are samples:

Your uncle has died, leaving you $10,000 in cash.

Your uncle has died, leaving you $50,000 in cash.

Your uncle has died, leaving you $100,000 in cash.

Your uncle has died, leaving you $500,000 in cash.

Under the terms of your late uncle's will you are to receive an annuity of $1,000 for as long as you live.

Under the terms of your late uncle's will you are to receive an annuity of $2,000 for as long as you live.

Under the terms of your late uncle's will you are to receive an annuity of $5,000 for as long as you live.

Under the terms of your late uncle's will you are to receive an annuity of $10,000 for as long as you live.

DECISION ITEMS

Prepare for each participant a collection of about twelve items on which decisions are to be made. If you are catering for a large number of people you will probably need to duplicate everything. For a small group, individual brochures and newspaper clippings may be included. It is not essential that the items in each collection be identical, though they should be similar. (For example, each participant might be given a different page from a catalogue of electrical appliances.) The following are examples of the kinds of things that might be included.

Brochures or advertisements for luxury goods, cars, travel, houses and holiday houses.

School prospectus and scale of fees.

Publicity material and/or advertisements relating to organizations and appeals such as Freedom From Hunger, Christmas Bowl, Save the Children, World Vision, denominational missions, etc.

A few personal letters and messages, as follows:

WARBURTON, WILLMORE & WARD
Investment Brokers

Dear

Our company specializes in all kinds of financial investment. We have had more than forty years experience in handling other people's money, to our mutual satisfaction.

If you are thinking of investing any money, it would be our pleasure to make all the necessary arrangements. We find that many people would like to put their money to work for them, but don't know where to start (or what stocks to buy).

People have all kinds of reasons for investing — and differing expectations. For some, it is long-term security that matters. They want dependable stock that will pay a steady, modest dividend. Others are after fast action right now, and they rely on us to get the best possible return for them at the least possible risk.

We don't yet know your needs, but we would like to meet with you and talk over your investment possibilities. If you are interested, please call our Miss Cox for an appointment with one of our experienced representatives. If, when you call, you would like to mention the approximate amount you are thinking of investing and the kind of action you want, our representative will have a sample portfolio drawn up ready for discussion when you meet.

We look forward to being of service.

Yours sincerely,

Chas E. Willmore

CHARLES E. WILLMORE,
Vice-President.

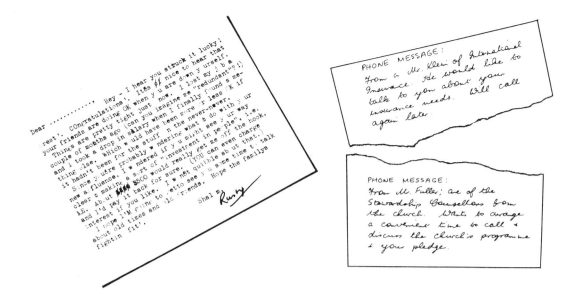

The decision items for each participant should be fastened with a paper clip.

Introducing the game

Explain briefly to the participants that they are to take part in a game concerned with the use of money.

Each person will participate as himself or herself. That is, each brings to the game his or her real circumstances and experiences in the way of family, possessions, debts, outlook on life, etc. Each person's starting point is where he is right now.

Distribute the SPREE SHEETS, one to each participant.

Give each participant a collection of decision items. Explain that some action must be taken on each item, and a note made on the SPREE SHEET. The order in which decisions are made ought also to be recorded. For example, one participant's first decision might be that he is not interested in buying a house, and his second might be that he would like to find out about insurance. On his SPREE SHEET he would write

1. house advertisement — WPB (wastepaper basket)

2. insurance — make appointment with rep.

Announce (or together decide upon) the time limit for decision-making. About 30 minutes should be sufficient.

Check that everyone understands the procedure and, if necessary, clarify.

After the game

Come together to share what has been done. With a large number of participants it is valuable to form groups of six to eight so that all may share in the discussion. Participants should discuss:

- what they did and why
- what decisions they found easy to make
- what decisions they found hard to make
- how the amount of money available influenced their decisions
- whether the windfall greatly affected their spending habits
- what else they would like to have done with the money.

Variations

In the form outlined above, SPREE! is an individual exercise. However, it could easily be adapted for family use at (say) a family camp. Instead of operating individually, families could discuss and make their decisions together. Similarly, it might be used as part of a youth/adult programme, with young people and their parents making family decisions together.

A game developed by the Section of Innovation and Experimentation (SINNEX) of the Division of the Local Church, The United Methodist Church, U.S.A.

"Swinging Into Mission" (SWIM) is a game to help planners in a local church experience and practice the following planning concepts:

- Programme as a means for achieving goals
- The variable effectiveness of programmes for achieving goals
- Cost-effectiveness as a criterion for selecting programme
- The priority weighting of goals
- The sequencing of programme in long-range planning.

In addition, it may be used to initiate actual planning. The last two rounds of the game lead into a consideration of next steps for the congregation's planners.

The goals and programmes of this game are related to an over-all objective for the congregation: "To extend and improve its mission of service and action in God's world".

NOTE: This game may be adapted for use in other organizations. First choose an over-all objective in keeping with the purpose of your organization (for example: to help your organization extend and improve its programme of fellowship, community service, and social action). Then adapt the goal and programme descriptions.

Playing the game

SWIM is designed to be played competitively between two or more teams of two to four (no more) SWIMMERS each. If possible, members of a team should be from the same congregation. The game may also be played competitively among two or more individual SWIMMERS, or non-competitively by one individual, several individuals, one team or several teams.

SWIM consists of four rounds, the Third round being the most difficult. The First, Second and Third Rounds are scored separately; there is no scoring for the Fourth Round.

The leader will

* Read in advance the four sheets of directions and see that each team receives a set

* See that each team receives a set of eight green Goal Cards and 24 yellow Programme Cards

* If desired, call time, post scores, and the like

* If desired, help SWIMMERS discuss the "possible learnings" related to each round.

Materials needed:

Set of four direction sheets for each team

Set of eight green Goal Cards for each team

Set of 24 yellow Programme Cards for each team.

DIRECTION SHEET 1 — FIRST ROUND

1. You and your teammates have an *objective:* to help your congregation extend and improve its mission of service and action in God's world. To reach that big objective you will need to reach certain smaller more manageable *goals.* Study the eight green Goal Cards. Select any two of these — goals that you would like to help your congregation achieve in the First Round. Set the other cards aside.

2. Now study briefly the 24 yellow Programme Cards. Note that each of these has "effectiveness" ratings from one to four for one or more goals. This represents the power of that programme to move your congregation toward the goal(s) indicated.

3. Pick out all those programmes that are effective in reaching either or both of your two goals. Set the other cards aside.

4. Now see how well you can reach your goals with only six programmes. That is, select those six Programme Cards that will give you the highest possible total effectiveness score in moving toward your two goals. Use the tally space below to work out your score.

Scoring

The team with the highest total effectiveness score for both its goals (combined) wins the First Round.

Tally

This is your work space. Enter your two goals. Then choose your programmes, writing in the large initial code letters and effectiveness scores for each. If you can improve your score, erase and enter other combinations.

PROGRAMMES   EFFECTIVENESS SCORES
(code letters)   1st goal: 2nd goal:
                                              _____   _____

_____   _____   _____
_____   _____   _____
_____   _____   _____
_____   _____   _____
_____   _____   _____
_____   _____   _____

                          TOTALS   _____   _____

                    COMBINED TOTAL   _____

Possible learnings

1. That programmes are a means for achieving goals. (We first select our goals — then programmes to reach them.)

2. That different programmes have various degrees of effectiveness for reaching intended goals. (Other things being equal, we choose the most effective programmes.)

3. That this game is rigged.

DIRECTION SHEET 2 — SECOND ROUND

1. With your teammates, select from among the green Goal Cards two new goals that you would like to achieve in this round. Set the other cards aside.

2. Now find those programmes that are effective in reaching these two goals. Pick out all such Programme Cards and set the others aside.

3. Note that each of these programmes "costs" something — in dollars and/or in the number of leader hours required to plan and carry it out.

4. See how well you can reach your two goals with only 250 cost units to spend. That is, which programmes with a total cost of no more than 250 hours-plus-dollars will give you the highest possible total effectiveness score in moving toward your goals? Use the tally space to work out alternatives and decide on the best combination.

Scoring

The team with the highest total effectiveness score wins (so long as it doesn't spend more than 250 cost units).

Tally

PROGRAMMES (code letters)	EFFECTIVENESS SCORES 1st goal:	2nd goal:	COST Dollars	Hours
_____	_____	_____	___	___
_____	_____	_____	___	___
_____	_____	_____	___	___
_____	_____	_____	___	___
_____	_____	_____	___	___
_____	_____	_____	___	___
_____	_____	_____	___	___
_____	_____	_____	___	___
_____	_____	_____	___	___
_____	_____	_____	___	___
_____	_____	_____	___	___
TOTALS	_____	_____	___	___
COMBINED TOTALS	_____		___	

Possible learnings

1. That you can't get something for nothing. (In choosing ways to reach our goals we count various costs.)

2. That *effectiveness relative to cost* is an important criterion for programme decisions. (We select programmes with the best "cost-effectiveness" ratio.)

3. That this game is getting tougher.

G

DIRECTION SHEET 3 — THIRD ROUND

1. Together consider your particular congregation's need and opportunity for discovering and moving into its mission. What are its present strengths and weaknesses? Then, using the green Goal Cards, choose those six goals that your congregation most needs to achieve.

2. Now give some priorities to these six goals.
   - Which two do you need to work especially hard on? These are your top priority goals; you must develop programmes with a total effectiveness of at least eight for each of these.
   - Which two goals have a middle priority? They each must be achieved to a minimum effectiveness of six.
   - And which two have low priority? They each must be achieved to a minimum effectiveness of four.
   Enter these six goals in the appropriate blanks of the tally space.

3. Now find programmes to achieve these goals equal to or exceeding the minimums. That would be easy, except for one thing: you have only 450 cost units (dollars-plus-hours) to spend! Lots of luck!

Scoring

The team with the highest total of effectiveness score wins (so long as it reaches each of the six minimums and does not spend more than 450 cost units).

Tally

PROGRAMMES	Top goals:		Middle goals:		Low goals:		COST $	Hours
	— —		— —		— —			
—	—	—	—	—	—	—	—	—
—	—	—	—	—	—	—	—	—
—	—	—	—	—	—	—	—	—
—	—	—	—	—	—	—	—	—
—	—	—	—	—	—	—	—	—
—	—	—	—	—	—	—	—	—
—	—	—	—	—	—	—	—	—
—	—	—	—	—	—	—	—	—
—	—	—	—	—	—	—	—	—
—	—	—	—	—	—	—	—	—
—	—	—	—	—	—	—	—	—
—	—	—	—	—	—	—	—	—
TOTALS	—	—	—	—	—	—	—	—
COMBINED TOTALS			———				——	

Possible learnings

1. That various goals have various priorities. (We weight our chosen goals according to need and significance.)

2. That, when standards must be met but resources are limited, *effectiveness relative to cost* is an *essential* criterion for programme decisions. (We develop that total programme that has the best cost-effectiveness ratio.)

3. That whoever invented this game was out of his skull.

DIRECTION SHEET 4 — FOURTH ROUND

1. Probably you have had enough of arithmetic for a while! You will welcome taking a different approach for this round. Lay the Goal Cards and Programme Cards you selected in the Third Round before you and study them. Then develop a one-year sequence of programmes by arranging the Programme Cards from left (how) to right (a year from now).

2. Here is a work space for sketching our your programme design for a year. Enter at the right the six goals you are seeking. Enter the twelve months for which you are planning. Then, using the Programme Card code letters, map our your programme sequence. Use lines, arrows, etc. to indicate how various programmes are related.

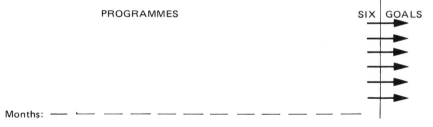

PROGRAMMES   SIX | GOALS

Months: — ·— — — — — — — — — — —

3. There is no scoring for this round. Rather, take some time to step out of the "game" spirit in which you have been participating and test this plan with one another. Are there parts of it that you would like to help your congregation implement? How can you do that? What first steps can you take right now?

Possible learnings

1. That some things *must* be done before other things *can* be done. (We schedule our programmes in a developmental sequence.)

2. That planning ahead is possible. (We plan now to reach goals that are a year or more distant.)

3. That cost-effectiveness planning is a lot of work, but may be worth it.

GOAL CARDS

Duplicate these on green card or paper.

MOTIVATION
Members of the congregation are excited about service and action as Christians in the world and are eager to extend and improve their ministries.

FOCUS
Members and groups in the congregation have identified certain specific issues or areas of ministry needing their attention.

INFORMATION
Members of the congregation have the knowledge regarding needs, resources, methods, etc. that is required for decision and action.

ORGANIZATION
The congregation is organized for effective study, decision, implementation, and evaluation of concrete ministries in the world.

TEAMWORK
Members and groups of the congregation are open, trusting, and accepting with one another and have a sense of unity in mission.

THEOLOGY
Members of the congregation understand and can describe their ministries as Christian responses to human need and God's work in the world.

SKILL
Members of the congregation have the various skills needed for planning together and carrying out ministries of service and action.

COOPERATION
Representatives of the congregation plan and implement the church's mission in cooperation with other congregations, other denominations and faiths, and other community agencies.

PROGRAMME CARDS

Duplicate these on yellow card or paper.

COOPERATIVE COMMUNITY-WIDE ACTIVITIES TO TRAIN CHURCHMEN IN SPECIFIC FORMS OF SERVICE

EFFECTIVENESS		COST
Cooperation	− 2	30 dollars
Skill	− 3	20 leader hours

A BULLETIN BOARD HIGHLIGHTING CURRENT ISSUES AND PROVIDING INFORMATION

EFFECTIVENESS		COST
Focus	− 1	20 leader hours
Information	− 1	

REGULAR CONSIDERATION IN THE LOCAL EDUCATION COMMITTEE OF THE WORK OF STUDY-ACTION TASK FORCES

EFFECTIVENESS		COST
Focus	− 1	20 leader hours
Information	− 1	

A FIVE-SESSION STUDY OF COMMUNITY DILEMMAS NEEDING THE RESPONSE OF CHRISTIANS

EFFECTIVENESS		COST
Motivation	− 2	30 dollars
Focus	− 1	30 leader hours
Information	− 3	

CHURCH MEMBERSHIP TRAINING FOCUSED ON ENLISTMENT IN THE CHURCH'S MISSION

EFFECTIVENESS		COST
Motivation	− 1	40 leader hours
Teamwork	− 2	
Organization	− 2	

A VIEWING AND DISCUSSION OF A FILM SHOWING SERVICE AND ACTION UNDERTAKEN BY OTHER GROUPS

EFFECTIVENESS		COST
Motivation	− 2	10 dollars
		10 leader hours

FIVE TRAINING SESSIONS IN GROUP AND INTER-PERSONAL RELATIONS FOR TASK FORCE MEMBERS

EFFECTIVENESS		COST
Teamwork	− 3	20 dollars
Skill	− 3	30 leader hours

MEMBERS OF THE CONGREGATION
HELPING THE COUNCIL OF CHURCHES
DEVELOP AN ACTION PROJECT

EFFECTIVENESS		COST
Cooperation	− 3	30 dollars
		10 leader hours

INTERVIEWS WITH STAFF OF SERVICE
AGENCIES IN THE COMMUNITY

EFFECTIVENESS		COST
Focus	− 2	30 leader hours
Information	− 2	
Cooperation	− 1	

SUBSCRIPTIONS FOR LEADERS TO
SEVERAL THEOLOGICAL **J**OURNALS

EFFECTIVENESS		COST
Theology	− 2	20 dollars

KEY MEMBERS OF THE CONGREGA-
TION APPOINTED TO SPECIAL INVESTI-
GATION IN VARIOUS AREAS

EFFECTIVENESS		COST
Focus	− 2	20 leader hours
Organization	− 2	

A CIRCULATING **L**IBRARY OF BOOKS
AND ARTICLES ON THE CHURCH AND
ITS MISSION

EFFECTIVENESS		COST
Theology	− 2	30 dollars

A **M**AILING TO THE CONGREGATION
OF REPRINTS DESCRIBING AND ANA-
LYZING PROBLEMS

EFFECTIVENESS		COST
Focus	− 1	10 dollars
Information	− 1	10 leader hours

STUDY OF **N**EW APPROACHES IN
SERVICE AND ACTION UNDERTAKEN
BY OTHER GROUPS

EFFECTIVENESS		COST
Information	− 2	30 leader hours
Cooperation	− 1	

A SATURDAY **O**BSERVATION TRIP
INTO AREAS OF NEED, AND INTERVIEWS
THERE

EFFECTIVENESS		COST
Focus	− 2	20 dollars
Motivation	− 2	20 leader hours
Information	− 2	

FIVE TRAINING SESSIONS IN
PROBLEM SOLVING AND ACTION
FOR TASK FORCE MEMBERS

EFFECTIVENESS		COST
Teamwork	− 2	30 dollars
Information	− 1	30 leader hours
Skill	− 4	

QUARTERLY WORKSHOPS OF MEM-
BERS OF THE CONGREGATION TO
PRACTICE THEIR SERVICE SKILLS

EFFECTIVENESS		COST
Skill	− 2	20 leader hours

THE CONGREGATION'S **R**EPRESENTA-
TIVES SERVING ON A CIVIC COMMITTEE
DEALING WITH A MAJOR ISSUE

EFFECTIVENESS		COST
Organization	− 1	30 dollars
Cooperation	− 3	10 leader hours

A SERIES OF FIVE **S**ERMONS ON THE
MISSION OF THE CHURCH WITH "TALK-
BACK" DISCUSSION

EFFECTIVENESS		COST
Motivation	− 2	60 leader hours
Theology	− 2	
Information	− 1	

ORGANIZATION AND MAINTENANCE
OF THREE INTER-CONGREGATIONAL
STUDY-ACTION **T**ASK FORCES

EFFECTIVENESS		COST
Teamwork	− 2	30 dollars
Focus	− 2	50 leader hours
Organization	− 3	
Cooperation	− 2	

A FIVE-SESSION **U**NIT OF STUDY ON BIBLICAL AND THEOLOGICAL FOUNDATIONS FOR MISSION

EFFECTIVENESS		COST
Motivation	— 2	30 dollars
Theology	— 3	30 leader hours

VOLUNTEERS FROM THE CONGREGATION LINKED WITH APPROPRIATE AGENCIES FOR SERVICE

EFFECTIVENESS		COST
Cooperation	— 3	40 leader hours
Skill	— 2	

A **W**EEKEND RETREAT FOR THE CONGREGATION'S OFFICERS TO SET GOALS FOR MISSION

EFFECTIVENESS		COST
Teamwork	— 1	30 dollars
Focus	— 2	20 leader hours
Organization	— 2	

A **Y**EAR OF STUDY BY THE CONGREGATION'S OFFICERS ON THE NATURE AND MISSION OF THE CHURCH

EFFECTIVENESS		COST
Motivation	— 2	20 dollars
Teamwork	— 3	50 leader hours
Theology	— 3	

THE POPULATION BOMB

A simulation game for examining the population crisis. Adapted from a report of an innovation in church education published by the Division of the Local Church, Board of Education of The United Methodist Church.

Any number of people may participate. They are divided into groups of 8–10.

If desired, you may begin by reading aloud the following two biblical passages: Genesis 1:26-31 and Psalm 8, using them to give a short exposition of some of the biblical and theological reasons why the church must be dealing creatively and responsibly with such problems as population.

Each player is given an instruction sheet with the following information:

THE POPULATION BOMB

The world is facing an international crisis in 1980. There simply is not enough food to feed everyone in Australia. Most of the rest of the world is starving. You have been appointed by the Prime Minister to serve on an emergency committee which will set priorities for our country in the next decade. You must decide what will be most useful in stemming the crisis in our nation and in the world.

Phase One

Prepare individually for the meeting of the committee by examining and ranking a series of priorities. Rank no. 1 the priority you think is most important, no. 2 the next most important, and so on.

Phase Two

Meet with other members of the committee to establish joint priorities. Attempt to do this by consensus, not by voting.

* * * * * *

Evaluation

Meet together for discussion at the end of the game. Did any of the committees succeed in establishing joint priorities? Were all members satisfied? What frustrations were experienced? What issues remained unresolved? Which received higher priority — practical moves (e.g., M, N) or high ideals e.g., G, H)?

THE PRIORITIES:

........A. Substantial cash grants for people who have no children. ....

........B. Opportunity to breathe clean air and drink fresh water. ....

........C. Stringent controls on pesticides to ensure safety. ....

........D. Voluntary family planning with a suggested limit of two children. ....

........E. National Parks providing facilities for camping, fishing, bush walking. ....

........F. Laws to safeguard principle that all are entitled to space for own home and small garden. ....

........G. Enough food in the world so that no one is hungry. ....

........H. Enough food in Australia so that no Australian is hungry. ....

.........I. Required sterilization of all males after two children. ....

........J. Freedom from thermonuclear war. ....

........K. Laws to safeguard individual right to have as many children as you want. ....

........L. Legalize voluntary euthanasia. ....

........M. Conservation of space by concentration on apartment blocks and community living quarters. ....

........N. Free contraceptives regularly issued to all females of child-bearing age. ....

........O. Laws to safeguard principle that all have the right to move about freely. ....

YOUTH WORK CARD SORT

An exercise for youth leaders and planners, developed by Mary-Ruth Marshall.

The purpose of this exercise is to open the way for more effective youth work by enabling participants to identify factors responsible for inadequate youth work in their organization.

Materials needed

one set of PROBLEM CARDS for each participant

one set of CATEGORY CARDS for each participant

one RECORD SHEET for each participant

supply of blank PROBLEM CARDS

one GROUP RECORD SHEET (sheet of newsprint set out in same way as individual record sheets)

pens or pencils; crayon or felt-tipped pen

PROBLEM CARDS

1 **Communication gap**
   Failure in real communication between youth and adults, and between youth and youth.

2 **Poor leadership**
   Untrained leaders preparing poorly, misunderstanding the objective, misusing materials and relying on impersonal, stereotyped, non-educational procedures.

3 **Uncommitted leadership**
   Workers who are vague about their identity as leaders and lukewarm about their leadership role.

4 **Irrelevancy**
   Leaders, setting, programmes, materials that seem unrelated to the individual's real world.

5 **Middle class mentality**
   Little concern for the unemployed, illiterate, culturally deprived, or for the intellectual and the artist.

6 **Obsession with organization**
   Excessive emphasis on organization, administration, and maintenance of the institution.

7 **Under-organization**
   Inadequate organization to plan, administer, supervise, evaluate the programme.

8 **Poor facilities**
   Overcrowded rooms, unattractive and non-functional settings, and inadequate equipment and supplies.

9 **Poor schedules**
   Insufficient time for all parts of the programme, simultaneous scheduling of activities, failure to make imaginative use of available time.

10 **Disunity**
   Lack of coordination in the organization's life and work, and sometimes competition among various programmes and groups.

11 **Disregard for absentees**
   Lack of systematic and concerned follow-up on absences.

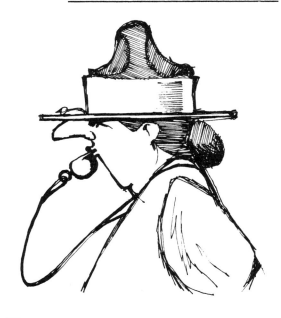

12 Lack of support for leaders
Organization, parents, and community fail to assist and appreciate youth workers.

13 Detached civic leaders
Nonsupport from civic leaders for group's work and, sometimes, alienation between community and civic leaders.

14 Noncooperative families
Parents who have no grasp of or concern for objective of the group and who do not support its programme.

15 Lack of goals
Aims confused, often unstated; lack of clarity in goals, or planning in terms of goal achievement. Inadequate evaluation.

16 Inadequate records
Failure to maintain a permanent roll or to record attendance.

17 Programme uniformity
Tendency to define and promote standard programmes and ways of organizing for all groups in spite of great variety of situations.

18 Lack of purpose
Work that is ingrown, self-serving, building-centred, status quo oriented and which, therefore, though it escapes all the other inadequacies, may still fail to serve the community and its people.

CATEGORY CARDS

These should be a different colour from the problem cards, since they are to be used as headings and should be easily distinguishable.

1
One most urgent problem:

2
Four next most urgent problems:

3
Eight more or less urgent problems:

4
Four less urgent problems:

5
One least urgent problem:

RECORD SHEET

1. One most urgent problem
2. Four next most urgent problems
3. Eight more or less urgent problems
4. Four less urgent problems
5. One least urgent problem

Procedure

1. Outline the purpose of the exercise.

2. Give each participant a set of problem and category cards. Say that the problems are those responsible for inadequate youth work in various organizations. They have been gathered from youth work surveys. Some will obviously be more responsible than others for any inadequacies in *your* youth work. The task of the participants is to sort the problem cards and place each one in its appropriate place below one of the category cards (these are laid out in numerical order as headings). Participants should note that the problems are to be ranked according to their relative urgency as responsible for inadequate youth work in your organization. Categories 4 and 5, therefore, will be the least serious problems — or things that are not your particular problem at all. If there is a problem omitted which any participant feels is responsible in your situation, he may write it on a blank problem card, substituting it for the problem he feels is most inappropriate. Participants will work alone.

3. Check that this part of the process is understood. Participants begin sorting.

4. Give each participant a record sheet on which to record the results of his card sort.

5. Participants move into small groups (3–6), to compare the results of their individual card sort. Participants may attempt to talk other members of the group into adopting the same categories. Allow about 5 minutes for sharing. At the end of this time, anyone who wishes to do so may alter his record sheet.

6. Come together to record results. On the group record sheet, record all the numbers listed in category 1 (with the number of "votes" for each); then those in categories 2, 3, 4, and 5.

7. What factors appear most consistently in categories 1 and 2? What can be done to reduce or eliminate them?

6
Doing your own thing

Most people who get enthusiastic about games and gaming soon want to produce games of their own. Two ways are open: (a) adaptation of existing games; (b) starting from scratch in developing new games. One of the advantages of the games technique is that the materials are flexible and easy to adapt. Just as you change other resources to meet the needs of your own situation, you'll discover ways of tailoring games to meet your specifications or needs.

Adaptation

It was the writer of Ecclesiastes who observed that "there is nothing new under the sun" (Ecclesiastes 1:9), and many simulation games seem to bear him out. There are a few basic designs which appear again and again with different trimmings. This is not to criticize — simply to point out that some game designs are particularly suited to adaptation.

The "survival" family of games has many adaptations. The original is probably "Lost on the Moon", an exercise developed by Jay Hall with the help of NASA. This game consists of ranking priorities, usually within some time limit or other constraint; it is often used to explore the area of consensus-reaching. "Survival Shelter" (p. 71) and "The Population Bomb" (p. 83) are both variations of this game.

In adapting this game yourself, you would need to list (or perhaps ask players to list) factors, conditions, components, or other elements which might be ranked according to priority. To make it a game, you would then need to create some story or theme in which to set the listing.

For example, with a group of young people, you might call the game "Utopia". The list could be of people, possessions, and/or principles for an ideal world. (This is a variation of the old "What Would You Take To A Desert Island?" game.) Using the game for teacher training, you might list various education resources which must be put into a shopping list according to priorities. In fact, there is such a game; it is called "Teacher Survival" and one form of it is to be found in Teachers' Training Kit No. 6, "Towards More Effective Use of the Christian Life Curriculum", published by the Joint Board of Christian Education.

Another very flexible form is the "In-Basket" type of game, of which "Spree!" (page 72) is an example. Originally intended for management training, it has been used effectively in teacher training and would readily lend itself to any kind of training programme concerned with decision-making responsibility and skills (for example, teachers, club or camp leaders, administrators). It simply needs an appropriate collection of items for the "in-basket".

If you wished to use this with youth leaders, for instance, you might include a number of letters, phone calls and messages which make demands on the leaders' time. Or for Sunday School teachers, fill the "in-basket" with questions, problems, challenging opportunities, crises, or interruptions, all of which must be dealt with in the class time.

Board games of the "Monopoly" style are easy to play and easy to adapt. In achieving the desired goal, players experience a model of a life situation. Chance devices, reflecting life as it is, affect the moves and outcomes of the players. "Getting There!", "Mana", "The Convict Game" and "Poor Man's Cake-Walk" (pages 40-58) are all of this genre. Board games from overseas sources are often not usable here in their original form. "Mana" is a New Zealand adaptation of the Friendship Press game, "Dignity"; in turn, "Mana" needs further alteration for Australian use.

As this is possibly the easiest kind of game to adapt, it may be the first one you will try. What about an adaptation of "Mana" which highlights the problems and difficulties of getting through secondary school successfully? Or, as appeared in idea form in the Sydney Alternative Pink Pages, an adaptation of "Monopoly" in which churches and other religious organizations seek to amass property, shares, and influence with government, while paying little or no rates and demanding several privileges.

The "Thumbs Up!" family of games, in which players must give answers to real-life problems and be assessed by other players on their answers, is another useful training aid. "Christlifestyle" (page 66) and "Camp Leaders' Training Game" (page 68) are both variations of this form.

Adaptation is simply a matter of asking players to write problems or areas of concern onto cards or paper. It is sometimes useful (as in the case of training youth leaders, for instance) to suggest that one be a personal problem and the other a professional or leadership one. Using this game with young people and their parents, or any other group with a communications difficulty, you might ask parents to deal with the young people's expressed problems, and vice versa.

Role-playing games in which tension is deliberately introduced are particularly useful for helping groups understand the feelings and situations of other people. "I'm Superior", "Arms Race", "Poverty", "Crisis in the Church", "Crystal Pistol", "The Gap", "Immigrants", "The Milk Run", "Project Economy" and "Family Charades" (pages 12-36) are all variations of this approach. Adaptation of this type of game is more likely to take the form which Dennis Benson calls "mind flints": ideas of ways to use this form in your own situation will be sparked off by playing the games or reading their descriptions.

Starting from scratch

Developing an entirely new game is usually far more difficult than adapting an existing one. It is something which ought not to be attempted until you have had some experience in playing existing games. Your first efforts will probably be imperfect, but you will likely learn as much from planning and developing an unfinished product as from using a ready-made one.

Game designing is an activity which has great possibilities as a group activity. Most of those described in Dennis Benson's book were developed in this way. If group members are prepared to put the time and energy needed into the task, designing a game about stewardship, career choices, attitudes to authority, or pollution and conservation could be one of the best ways of learning about the subject.

Initially the ideas for the game may come in a kind of haphazard, brainstorming way, but sooner or later you will need to work through them in a more systematic manner. The following steps, developed by an experienced game designer (Clark C. Abt of Abt Associates) provide a sound pattern for game development:

1. Define your *objectives*. State what you want to teach or want the group to learn/understand/feel through the game. Try to set the objectives out in terms of what you hope the participants will be able to do after the game.

2. Decide on the *scope* of the game. Choose the time, place and issues to be represented. Try to find a simple model of the process or system which best serves your objective.

3. Identify key *players*. Players, actors or teams may represent individuals, groups, organizations, or

institutions. Housekeeping functions such as banker, messenger, or game director may need to be included. Decide which forces are to be mechanized by some form of chance device and which ones will be represented by human players.

4. Decide players' *goals*. Define their objectives clearly and provide some means of implementing them. One form is: "Your goal is to get as much....... as you can without being .... or losing ...."

5. Decide what *resources* players will have. This may include money, power, information, votes, troops, etc. There will be tangible assets such as money, and intangible ones such as social position. Give a precise value to all resources so that success or failure can be determined at given points and at the end of the game.

6. Decide how the *interaction* between players will take place. Determine if there will be "rounds" in the game, and how they will be organized. The sequence cycle you choose will give structure to the game. Make it clear what has to be done in the game.

7. Decide the *rules* which will govern decision-making in the game. Determine what is permissible behaviour. Set time limits for various stages or rounds in the game. Rules should embody real-life limitations and should be phrased in real-life terms. Run through the players' roles and think of what you would do if there were no rules. Try to find loopholes; decide if they should exist and provision accordingly.

8. Identify external *constraints.* Actions open to the players must be realistic in terms of the situation being represented. For example, in a game about conflict in a youth group, members of the group would not plot to murder the leader!

9. Set out rules for *scoring* and winning. Define win criteria in terms of the players' objectives. The degree to which players achieve their goals is measurement of who wins. You may wish to translate intangibles into points or money. If a number of players achieve their goals, you may name as winner the one who does so first.

10. Decide on the *format* best suited to the game. You may choose between board game, role-play, pencil and paper, card sort or other such exercise, or some combination of these. Where the process is clearly described, some form of gameboard is useful to record action. You may use individual boards or one larger one. (A theatre game developed for English schools utilizes one board which covers the entire floor space; players become their own counters.) Boards are best used when the subject matter and variables are concrete and easily measured. Where the discussion of issues based on written profiles is the substance of the game, where "human factors" are paramount, a board is unnecessary.

Though decisions about format and rules are the last steps in game design, it is good to have them in mind as you work through the designing process. You may find you will wish to return to Step 1 and recycle the planning. Have a dry run session with friends or a volunteer group, checking particularly to see that the game represents reality and relates specifically to your objectives from Step 1. No matter how enjoyable or fascinating your game is, if it isn't "real" or is not clearly related to your objectives, it is of little use.

Game materials

Whether you are adapting existing games or creating new ones, there are a few things you will need to know about game materials. Three items which call for considerable attention are chance devices, scenarios, and role profiles.

CHANCE DEVICES. All board games and many role-play and hybrid games need some means of introducing chance factors. Such devices are customarily used to represent Nature or fate in a game. If it is simply a matter of determining the number of spaces a counter is to be advanced on a board, a die or pair of dice is all that is needed. Other chance factors may be introduced by means of spinners, chance cards, random numbers table, flipping a coin, etc.

SCENARIOS. In a role-play game, the scenario sets the scene for the game action. It is a briefing on the situation right up to the moment of the game. It should be concise but informative, including a statement of the issue at stake and an outline of its historical background. This will comprise only what would be common knowledge to all players. Some of the rules of the game will probably be included; for example, communications restraints.

ROLE-PROFILES. Role-profiles should be prepared with care. They should include precise objectives for the player or players in question. Role-profiles are usually written in the second person. Sometimes profiles are provided for individual players; in other cases, the profiles are applicable to the groups in which the players operate. As well as the goals or objectives, the profile should include the person's or group's position in the situation, his/their attitude, information about the situation available only to that person or group, and some hints about behaviour, particularly for the early stages of the game. Participants may sometimes be asked to write their own role-profiles, given basic information such as name, age, occupation (possibly), and general attitude to the situation.

Sometimes the scenario is combined with the role profile. A good example of this is found in the game called "Crunch" in Dennis Benson's *Gaming.* "Crunch" is an international relations game, and the representatives of each nation receive a background document written from the viewpoint of their country. For the most part, the information is the same for each country, but it is slanted in a particular way. Which is realistic, when you come to think of it.

Other game materials may vary according to what is available, cost, and the amount of storage space you have. Some easily available materials for making your own game model are:

GAMEBOARDS
Sheets of graph paper or newsprint
Poster board (partially slit with razor, tape hinge on reverse side, for foldability)
Non-patterned or clear oilcloth) makes a rollable
Clear plastic film or shower) easy to clean
curtaining) gameboard
Clear Contact)

DECORATING GAMEBOARDS
Felt-tip pens
Paints (artist's colours will not smear)
Gummed paper
Gummed circles, squares, stars, etc.
Letra-set figures and letters
Letters and figures cut from newspapers and magazines.

CHANCE DEVICES
Dice
Spinner
Coloured systems cards for chance cards
Coin

TOKENS, RESOURCE SYMBOLS
Toy miniatures (tiny cars, animals, etc.)
Wooden blocks or beads in assorted colours
Poker chips
Costume jewellry
Play money
Assorted coins

PLAYER IDENTIFICATION
Name tags or labels
Badges
Armbands

OTHER
Bell or whistle to signal end of round, special announcements, etc.
Stop watch, watch with second hand or clock
Pencils or biros

Mind flints

Dennis Benson's book *Gaming* has a chapter which he calls "mind flints": raw ideas which strike sparks when rubbed against people doing a particular task. He suggests that such raw ideas are all around, just waiting to be brought to life. Books, films, events, issues — all are possible sources of game ideas.

At least two of the games described in *Gaming* were sparked off by books or films. "Ralph" came out of someone being "turned on" by *2001: A Space Odessey.* "Flight 108" grew out of a combination of the book *Situation Ethics* and various movies about air disasters.

Another group came up with a game called "The Widening Gap" after reading Barbara Ward's book, *The Lopsided World.* What books have you read lately that suggest ideas for games? What about *Future Shock? The Female Eunuch?*

What about movies or TV programmes? Have you been excited, maddened, disgusted by events that have made the news? Has a particular issue got under your skin? These are your mind flints, waiting to be struck.

A book for designers

If you are seriously interested in game design, you should get hold of a book which goes in for rather more detail than we have been able to give: Ray Glazer, *How to Design Educational Games* (Abt Associates, Inc., 1969).

Bibliography

The following books have been consulted in compiling this guide, and are recommended to those who would like to do more reading on the subject. Don't be put off if your bookseller doesn't have them in stock. Ask for them to be ordered. Try both educational and religious book shops.

Dennis Benson, *Gaming: The Fine Art of Creating Simulation/Learning Games for Religious Education* (Abingdon Press, 1971)
Ray Glazier, *How to Design Educational Games* (Abt Associates, Inc., 1969)
John L. Taylor and Rex Walford, *Simulation in the Classroom* (Penguin Papers in Education, 1972)
J. Wilbur Paterson, *Simulation Games* (The Geneva Press, 1969)
P.J. Tansey and Derick Unwin, *Simulation and Gaming in Education* (Methuen Education Limited, 1969)
William A. Nesbitt, *Simulation Games for the Social Studies Classroom* (Foreign Policy Association, 1971)
Alice Kaplan Gordon, *Games for Growth* (Science Research Associates, Inc., 1971)
Sarane S. Boocock and E.O. Schild (eds.), *Simulation Games In Learning,* (Sage Publications, Inc., 1968)
Donald E. Miller, Graydon F. Snyder, and Robert W. Neff, *Using Biblical Simulations* (Judson Press, 1973)
Dennis M. Adams, *Simulation Games: An Approach to Learning* (Charles A. Jones, 1973)
Jeffrey Schrank, *Using Games in Religion Class* (Paulist Press, 1973)
Karen R. Krupar *Communication Games* Participant's Manual (The Free Press, 1973)